I0007490

Bare-Metal Rust Programming

**Build Reliable Firmware with Bare-Metal Rust
for Microcontrollers and Embedded Systems**

Jose Gobert

Table of Contents

Preface

Welcome, reader. If you've ever worked with embedded systems, you know how demanding they can be. Whether you're developing firmware for a tiny temperature sensor or a complex microcontroller-based automation system, the need for precision, safety, and reliability is non-negotiable. Mistakes in firmware often lead to bugs that are difficult to trace, unpredictable behaviors in critical systems, and in some cases, hardware damage or safety hazards. This book is written with a singular goal: to show you how Rust can be used to build robust, maintainable, and safe firmware for bare-metal systems.

Embedded systems have traditionally been built using C or C++—languages that offer low-level control and performance, but also come with a long history of security vulnerabilities and undefined behavior due to things like buffer overflows, null pointer dereferencing, and data races. These issues persist not because developers are careless, but because the languages themselves do not actively prevent them.

Rust is different. It's a systems programming language that provides the same low-level access to hardware as C, but with a strong focus on safety and correctness. Its ownership model, type system, and strict compile-time checks make entire classes of bugs impossible to express. For bare-metal firmware— where there's no operating system to catch mistakes and where every byte and clock cycle matters—Rust gives you the control you need without sacrificing safety.

This book focuses specifically on *bare-metal Rust*, meaning that we'll be working directly with hardware, without the support of an operating system or runtime. This requires a unique way of thinking about program structure, memory layout, and hardware interaction. It also offers the opportunity to write firmware that is predictable, efficient, and deeply reliable.

Who This Book Is For

This book is written for embedded systems developers who are curious about Rust, as well as Rust developers who are interested in working closer to the hardware. If you're coming from a background in C or C++ firmware development, you'll find that Rust offers familiar concepts with modern safeguards. If you're a Rust developer looking to apply your skills in embedded contexts, you'll gain the practical knowledge needed to build real firmware for microcontrollers.

You don't need to be an expert in embedded systems to benefit from this book. If you've never written firmware before, but you're comfortable with Rust or another programming language and you're curious about working at the hardware level, this book will help you understand how to get started the right way. If you're already experienced in embedded development, this book will show you how to apply your knowledge using safer, more modern tools.

What You'll Learn and Build

You'll start by learning how to configure a Rust project for bare-metal development using `no_std`, which refers to Rust code that runs without the standard library. This is essential for systems where no operating system exists. You'll understand how to use the `core` library, which provides fundamental functionality such as mathematical operations, basic data types, and formatting without relying on OS-level services.

As the book progresses, you'll build real programs that run directly on microcontroller hardware. You'll blink LEDs, configure timers, respond to interrupts, and communicate over protocols like UART, I2C, and SPI. These aren't just toy examples—they represent the foundational building blocks of nearly all embedded systems.

You'll also learn how to structure firmware for scalability and reusability using Rust's trait system and module organization. Along the way, we'll explore how to debug firmware with modern tools like `probe-rs`, how to optimize binaries for size and performance, and how to design firmware that's robust in production environments.

By the end of this book, you will have a strong grasp of how to write bare-metal firmware in Rust, grounded in both theoretical understanding and practical experience.

Required Knowledge and Tools

To get the most out of this book, you should have some familiarity with programming concepts such as variables, functions, and control flow. A basic understanding of the Rust language—how ownership and borrowing work, how to define structs and traits, and how to write generic code—will be helpful. If you're new to Rust, you may want to first work through *The Rust Programming Language* (commonly called "The Book"), which is freely available online.

In terms of tooling, you'll need the Rust compiler, `cargo` (Rust's package manager and build system), and some additional tools like `probe-rs` for flashing and debugging. We'll walk through installing all of these in Chapter 2. You'll also need access to a development board based on a supported microcontroller architecture. Boards based on ARM Cortex-M chips are ideal for this book, and affordable options like the STM32, nRF52, or RP2040 will work perfectly.

You'll be writing code that runs directly on hardware, so a USB debugger or debug probe will also be useful. Many development boards include this built-in, but we'll cover your options clearly when we reach the hardware setup phase.

Ultimately, all you need is a curiosity about how computers work at the lowest level, and a willingness to build something from the metal up. Let's begin.

Chapter 1: Rust in Embedded Systems

When you're writing firmware for embedded systems—code that lives closest to the hardware—your job is both critical and unforgiving. You're expected to produce binaries that are fast, efficient, and stable. Every byte counts. Every cycle matters. And one silent bug can mean the difference between a device that just works and one that fails unpredictably in the field. This is why so many embedded developers turn to languages like C and C++. They've been the standard for decades because they offer the low-level access required to interact directly with registers, memory, and peripherals. But with great power comes... lots of responsibility. And that responsibility often falls squarely on your shoulders when things go wrong.

Rust presents a compelling alternative—not by removing that power, but by giving you powerful tools to wield it more safely. It promises the same level of control you get from C, but with guarantees that can eliminate entire classes of bugs before your code even compiles. In this chapter, we'll talk about why Rust is gaining traction in the embedded space and what makes it such a strong candidate for firmware development.

Rust and C/C++ in Embedded Development

Let's have a frank discussion about the languages we use to control the lowest layers of computing: firmware. When building software that runs without an operating system—directly on bare metal—C and C++ are the historical heavyweights. They've been the default choice for decades, thanks to their low-level access, small footprint, and close mapping to machine instructions. If you're reading this, there's a good chance you've already written embedded code in one of them. They've earned their place, but they also come with well-documented problems, especially when it comes to reliability and maintainability.

Rust enters this space with the promise of solving those problems without giving up the control that makes C attractive. To fully appreciate what Rust brings to the table, we need to get specific about the strengths and weaknesses of each.

C gives you raw control. You define variables, manipulate pointers, write directly to memory-mapped registers, and control the execution flow without any abstraction in the way. It's efficient and predictable—but only if you know exactly what you're doing. One mistake, like writing past the end of an array, dereferencing a null pointer, or misaligning data in memory, can lead to hard-to-trace bugs or even catastrophic hardware behavior. There's no guardrail.

C++ builds on C by offering object-oriented features, generic programming with templates, and stronger type safety in some areas. But in embedded programming, many developers avoid the more complex features of C++ entirely. Why? Because they introduce unpredictability, increase binary size, and can lead to subtle bugs if you're not careful with things like virtual functions or dynamic memory. In real-time systems, deterministic behavior matters more than clever abstractions.

Rust offers the same level of control as C. You can write directly to memory-mapped registers. You can manipulate bitfields and configure peripherals with precision. But Rust adds safety and clarity where C and C++ leave gaps. For example, in Rust, variables are either owned, borrowed immutably, or borrowed mutably—but never more than one mutable borrow at a time. This eliminates a large category of bugs that C developers have to catch manually, like data races and use-after-free errors.

Let's take a practical example. Suppose you're writing to a GPIO register on a microcontroller to toggle an LED. In C, that might look like this:

```
#define GPIO_PORT (*(volatile unsigned
int*)0x48000014)
void toggle_led() {
    GPIO_PORT ^= (1 << 5);
}
```

This works fine, but it's dangerously flexible. You can write to that memory at any time, from anywhere in the code, with no checks in place.

Here's the same idea expressed in Rust using a `volatile` pointer with controlled access:

```
use core::ptr;

const GPIO_PORT: *mut u32 = 0x48000014 as *mut u32;
```

```
pub fn toggle_led() {
    unsafe {
        let val = ptr::read_volatile(GPIO_PORT);
        ptr::write_volatile(GPIO_PORT, val ^ (1 <<
5));
    }
}
```

In this Rust version, it's clear that we're doing something risky—unsafe makes that explicit. The compiler won't let this code run in safe Rust, and that's not a limitation—it's a signal. Rust forces you to isolate the code that breaks the usual safety guarantees, making it easier to audit and contain. In contrast, in C, every line of code is effectively "unsafe," but it never tells you that.

This small difference scales up. When working with shared memory in C, especially in interrupt-driven systems, you have to manually guard against race conditions. Rust requires you to use synchronization primitives like Mutex, or atomic types, and ensures at compile time that concurrent mutable access is never allowed without proper handling.

Let's say you have a global flag updated in an interrupt handler and read in your main loop. In C, this would be a volatile variable. But that's not enough to prevent race conditions or ensure atomicity.

In Rust, you might use an AtomicBool:

```
use core::sync::atomic::{AtomicBool, Ordering};

static LED_STATE: AtomicBool =
AtomicBool::new(false);

#[interrupt]
fn EXTI0() {
    LED_STATE.store(true, Ordering::Relaxed);
}

fn main_loop() {
    if LED_STATE.load(Ordering::Relaxed) {
        // do something
    }
}
```

This is safe, thread-aware, and obvious. You're forced to think about memory ordering and concurrency strategy, even in a single-core system where the main loop and ISRs are interleaved.

Another key area where Rust excels is in function signatures and type safety. In C, functions can return anything, or nothing, and parameters are loosely typed unless you're vigilant. In Rust, the compiler enforces clarity. A function returning a result that might fail must use `Result<T, E>`, so you're never allowed to ignore a failure unless you explicitly acknowledge it.

Here's an example of an SPI write operation using a HAL crate:

```
fn send_data<SPI: Write<u8>>(spi: &mut SPI, byte:
u8) {
    if let Err(e) = spi.write(&[byte]) {
        // Handle error, maybe log it or retry
    }
}
```

This makes error handling a first-class concern. You're not allowed to skip it. C, on the other hand, often leaves error detection and handling as optional, or worse—buried in documentation that many overlook.

Beyond safety and correctness, Rust offers modern tooling. The compiler gives incredibly helpful messages when you make a mistake. The package manager, `cargo`, handles builds, dependencies, and workspaces cleanly. Linting, formatting, and documentation tools are integrated and standardized. There's no fragmented ecosystem of third-party makefiles and custom build scripts as in many C projects.

And yet, despite all this safety and tooling, Rust still compiles to efficient, small binaries suitable for microcontrollers. With link-time optimization (LTO) and features like zero-cost abstractions, your Rust code can match or beat C performance while remaining more readable and easier to test.

In bare-metal programming, reliability is non-negotiable. Rust gives you the same direct access to hardware as C, but surrounds that access with guardrails, compiler-enforced discipline, and a better developer experience. It's not trying to replace C just for the sake of change—it's here to make firmware more robust and your job less error-prone. As you'll see throughout this book, once you've written firmware in Rust and seen the benefits for yourself, it's hard to go back.

Memory Safety and Concurrency

One of the most critical challenges in embedded systems programming is managing memory correctly. Unlike application-level development on desktops or servers, embedded systems often run without dynamic memory allocation, garbage collection, or even operating system-level memory protection. When you're working directly with raw pointers, memory-mapped peripherals, and interrupt-driven control flows, the margin for error is incredibly small.

In this environment, memory safety isn't just a bonus—it's the difference between a device that runs reliably in the field and one that silently corrupts data, crashes, or causes real-world harm. This is exactly where Rust's strongest features come into play: its approach to memory management and concurrency is built to give you control *and* safety, without sacrificing performance.

Let's start with what memory safety actually means in this context. In languages like C, it's your responsibility to ensure that every pointer you use is valid, that memory is properly initialized before it's accessed, and that you never read from or write to areas that don't belong to you. The compiler will not stop you from doing something unsafe. It assumes you know what you're doing—and when you get it wrong, the results can be subtle and devastating.

Rust, on the other hand, enforces memory safety at compile time. It tracks ownership of each piece of data, ensuring that there's exactly one owner at any given time, and that any references to that data are either read-only or mutable—but not both. This is enforced without any runtime overhead. If your code compiles, you've already passed a significant number of correctness checks.

To understand this, let's walk through a simple example. Suppose you're toggling an LED using a shared peripheral structure. In C, you'd typically use a `volatile` pointer and access it directly:

```
#define GPIO_PORT (*(volatile unsigned
int*)0x48000014)
void toggle_led() {
    GPIO_PORT ^= (1 << 5);
}
```

But what happens if two parts of your code—perhaps the main loop and an interrupt handler—both modify that register at the same time? You might end up with a race condition. The LED might not toggle as expected. Or worse, you might inadvertently clear or set other bits in that register.

Rust avoids this entirely by forcing you to make data access patterns explicit and safe. When sharing data between execution contexts—such as between an interrupt and the main loop—Rust won't let you have unsynchronized access. Here's how you might solve this using atomic types:

```rust
use core::sync::atomic::{AtomicU32, Ordering};

static GPIO_STATE: AtomicU32 = AtomicU32::new(0);

pub fn toggle_led() {
    let current =
GPIO_STATE.load(Ordering::Relaxed);
    GPIO_STATE.store(current ^ (1 << 5),
Ordering::Relaxed);
}
```

This version guarantees that the read and write to GPIO_STATE are atomic. If this value were used to control GPIO register settings, you'd know that concurrent access would be safe, even if one context is preempting the other.

For more complex data—such as a buffer or a structure holding device configuration—you can't just use atomic types. In those cases, Rust gives you tools like Mutex or critical section APIs. Here's a real-world embedded Rust pattern using critical-section to protect shared state:

```rust
use core::cell::RefCell;
use cortex_m::interrupt::Mutex;
use cortex_m_rt::entry;
use stm32f4xx_hal::pac::USART1;

static UART: Mutex<RefCell<Option<USART1>>> =
Mutex::new(RefCell::new(None));

#[interrupt]
fn USART1() {
    cortex_m::interrupt::free(|cs| {
```

```
        if let Some(ref mut uart) =
UART.borrow(cs).borrow_mut().as_mut() {
            // Handle UART interrupt safely
        }
    });
}
```

This pattern guarantees that access to the UART peripheral is synchronized and cannot be mutated simultaneously from the main context and an interrupt handler. The Mutex ensures exclusive access, and RefCell provides interior mutability—a safe way to allow mutability even when the outer variable is immutable, as long as it's properly synchronized.

Now let's consider the concept of use-after-free—a classic bug in C where a pointer is used after the memory it refers to has been deallocated. In bare-metal systems, you're often working with static memory, but in cases where you pass ownership or reuse buffers, this bug can still appear. Rust's ownership system eliminates this by design. Once ownership is transferred, the original variable is no longer valid:

```
fn take_ownership(data: Vec<u8>) {
    // `data` is now owned here
}

fn main() {
    let buffer = vec![1, 2, 3];
    take_ownership(buffer);
    // buffer is no longer accessible here
}
```

This may seem restrictive at first, but it forces you to write code that respects the boundaries of memory lifetime and access. In embedded development, where reliability is crucial, this is a major advantage.

Concurrency is another area where Rust changes the game. In C, handling concurrency correctly is largely a matter of discipline. You manually disable interrupts, implement double-buffering, or use volatile variables to hint to the compiler not to optimize out important reads or writes. Rust's type system lets you encode these patterns directly into your types and function signatures. The compiler then enforces them every time you use that code.

Let's say you're sharing a buffer between a DMA controller and your firmware. In Rust, you can use lifetimes to ensure the buffer is only used by one party at a time. If your API requires exclusive access (`&mut [u8]`), then you can be confident that nothing else is accessing it concurrently. If you pass it to the DMA driver, you can't use it again until the driver gives it back.

This kind of enforced discipline is essential in real-time systems. It's not just about avoiding bugs—it's about guaranteeing correctness under all possible execution paths. And when you're working with critical devices like motor controllers, medical equipment, or industrial sensors, that kind of guarantee isn't a luxury. It's the baseline.

Rust's memory safety and concurrency guarantees don't make embedded programming easy. You'll still need to understand how hardware works, how peripherals interact, and how interrupts behave. But what Rust does is remove an entire layer of uncertainty. It tells you when your assumptions about memory access or synchronization are wrong—at compile time, before those assumptions turn into expensive bugs in the field.

And once you've seen how much more confidence this gives you in your code, it stops feeling restrictive. It starts feeling like the way embedded programming should have worked all along.

Zero-Cost Abstractions and Performance

In embedded systems, every byte matters and every cycle counts. Whether you're writing firmware for a tiny battery-powered sensor or for a high-throughput motor controller, your software has to be efficient—not only in terms of memory usage, but also in terms of execution time and predictability. Historically, this is exactly why embedded developers have leaned on C. It's a minimal language. It gives you a direct path to the machine. But it also gives you nothing else. You're left to build or manage every abstraction yourself, and often, when you try to make your code cleaner or more reusable, you pay for it—both in terms of performance and binary size.

Rust does something fundamentally different. It lets you write high-level, expressive code—code that's modular, generic, and composable—and it gives you that for free, in terms of runtime performance. This is what we mean when we talk about *zero-cost abstractions*. You get the benefit of abstraction without the performance penalty typically associated with it.

Suppose you're writing a driver for a digital temperature sensor using the I²C protocol. In C, you might write a function that takes an I²C register address and writes to it. But that function is tightly coupled to whatever specific peripheral you're using, and you'll need to duplicate that logic or rewrite it entirely for another platform.

In Rust, you can define a trait that describes how I²C communication works—abstracting over the hardware—and then write your driver generically against that trait:

```
use embedded_hal::blocking::i2c::{Write, Read};

pub struct TempSensor<I2C> {
    i2c: I2C,
    address: u8,
}

impl<I2C, E> TempSensor<I2C>
where
    I2C: Write<Error = E> + Read<Error = E>,
{
    pub fn new(i2c: I2C, address: u8) -> Self {
        Self { i2c, address }
    }

    pub fn read_temp(&mut self) -> Result<u16, E> {
        let mut buffer = [0; 2];
        self.i2c.write(self.address, &[0x01])?;
        self.i2c.read(self.address, &mut buffer)?;
        Ok(u16::from_be_bytes(buffer))
    }
}
```

Here's the key point: even though this code is written generically, when you compile it for a specific platform, the compiler *monomorphizes* it. That means it generates concrete versions of this code for the actual I²C implementation you pass in. There's no virtual function call. There's no heap allocation. The result is machine code that is as efficient as hand-written C targeted to that specific peripheral.

This pattern is everywhere in Rust's embedded ecosystem. Abstractions are built using traits and generics, and those abstractions are compiled down into direct, efficient instructions. You get code reuse and modularity without introducing indirection or runtime cost.

Let's go even further. Suppose you write a reusable delay function using traits:

```
use embedded_hal::blocking::delay::DelayMs;

pub fn wait_for_sensor_ready<D:
DelayMs<u16>>(delay: &mut D) {
    delay.delay_ms(10);
}
```

This function is abstract over *how* the delay is implemented. It could be a busy-wait loop using a timer peripheral, or it could be a real-time OS sleep call, depending on the platform. But again, once this is compiled for a specific implementation of `DelayMs`, the generic call turns into a direct function call to the concrete implementation. There's no cost to writing the code in a general way.

Now let's contrast that with what you typically do in C. You might use a function pointer to create an interface. But that pointer indirection adds overhead, and it's up to you to make sure the function signatures match, the pointer is valid, and the performance trade-offs are acceptable. Rust handles all of this through its type system and compiler. It gives you the flexibility of abstraction without compromising execution efficiency.

Another place where zero-cost abstraction pays off is in embedded drivers and HAL crates. For example, the `stm32f4xx-hal` crate provides a GPIO abstraction that lets you configure pins as input or output, toggle them, and read their state, all in a safe and expressive way:

```
let gpioa = dp.GPIOA.split();
let mut led = gpioa.pa5.into_push_pull_output();

led.set_high().unwrap();
```

This code is built on top of strongly typed abstractions. The pin type knows its mode—input, output, analog—and the compiler won't let you call `set_high()` unless the pin is in an output mode. This kind of type-safe API would be tedious to enforce in C and would typically be omitted entirely in favor of simpler, unsafe macros. But in Rust, this safety comes with no runtime cost. The final assembly is a few direct register instructions to set or clear the pin.

And it's not just performance—it's predictability. In real-time systems, knowing *when* something will execute is just as important as knowing *what* it will do. Rust encourages designs where timing and logic are explicit. There's no garbage collector. There's no dynamic dispatch unless you ask for it. You know when code allocates, you know where it lives, and you know what it costs.

Let's also talk about binary size. There's a myth that Rust always produces large binaries. This only holds if you compile with default settings, pull in unnecessary crates, or forget to tune your build profile. With `opt-level = "z"`, link-time optimization, and stripping debug info, Rust binaries can be just as small as C binaries. For example, a blinking LED project targeting an STM32 microcontroller can produce a final binary well under 10 KB.

Here's a simple `Cargo.toml` tweak that helps:

```
[profile.release]
opt-level = "z"
lto = true
codegen-units = 1
panic = "abort"
```

With those settings, the compiler aggressively minimizes size, inlines code across crates, and avoids unnecessary panic machinery—all important for microcontrollers with 32 KB or 64 KB of flash.

The real power of zero-cost abstractions isn't that they make your code faster. It's that they let you write *better* code—cleaner, more modular, easier to test, and safer to maintain—*without* trading away performance. That's the trade-off C developers have had to make for decades. And it's a trade-off Rust eliminates.

Once you've written a few reusable drivers in Rust and watched the compiler turn them into tiny, efficient machine code with no dynamic overhead, you start to realize something: abstraction doesn't have to mean inefficiency. With the right tools and language design, you can have both. Rust gives you that—by design.

Real-World Adoption and Ecosystem Overview

Rust is no longer an experimental choice for systems programming. What began as a research project inside Mozilla has grown into a production-grade language used by companies, open-source communities, and hobbyists to build fast, reliable, and safe software. In the embedded systems space specifically, Rust has found a foothold in real-world use cases where safety and performance are equally critical—and where mistakes can't be tolerated.

Adoption in this field hasn't come about through hype. It's been the result of a growing recognition that Rust's guarantees solve the kinds of problems that embedded developers face every day: memory corruption, undefined behavior, data races, and debugging difficulties on resource-constrained devices. You'll find Rust now being used in areas as diverse as aerospace, medical devices, IoT hardware, robotics, and industrial control systems.

Let's start with a specific example. One of the more public adopters of Rust for embedded systems is the European Space Agency (ESA). Their software team explored the use of Rust in satellite firmware development, comparing it against traditional C-based approaches. They cited the memory safety guarantees, enforced concurrency models, and lack of runtime overhead as key reasons to continue with Rust. In space systems, the ability to detect errors at compile time rather than during field operation can be mission-critical—literally.

Another concrete case is the **Ferrocene project**, a commercial toolchain initiative by Ferrous Systems in collaboration with AdaCore. It aims to create a Rust toolchain that is qualified for safety-critical systems—think avionics, automotive (ISO 26262), and industrial control. That kind of certification takes years and heavy scrutiny, and yet it's happening for Rust. This tells you that organizations working with the most demanding safety standards see long-term value in building embedded systems in Rust.

Outside of high-assurance fields, startups and open-source hardware projects are also building products using embedded Rust. For instance, the open-source drone project *Ardupilot* has seen interest in integrating Rust-based modules for telemetry and safety features. Developers contributing to embedded platforms like the RP2040 (Raspberry Pi Pico) and the STM32 family frequently write HALs and drivers in Rust, often because of the clarity and reusability that Rust's type system enforces.

But real-world adoption is only half of the picture. The other half is the ecosystem—what tools are available, what libraries are maintained, and how easy it is for you to actually get work done.

At the foundation of embedded Rust is `no_std` support. This is the mode Rust uses when you don't have access to an operating system, standard I/O, heap allocation, or other runtime conveniences. In `no_std`, you're only using Rust's core language capabilities and the `core` crate, which provides essential types and operations—things like math, slices, iterators, and formatting.

Building on top of that is the **Rust Embedded Working Group**, which has produced a whole suite of crates that make it practical to build hardware-level software:

- `cortex-m` **and** `cortex-m-rt`: These crates give you low-level access to Cortex-M processor features, including exception handling, vector tables, and interrupts.
- `embedded-hal`: This crate defines a set of traits that abstract over common peripheral functions like GPIO, I2C, SPI, and UART. It allows you to write drivers that are platform-agnostic and reusable across different microcontroller architectures.
- **Peripheral Access Crates (PACs)**: Generated from vendor-supplied SVD files, these crates give you type-safe access to memory-mapped peripheral registers. For instance, `stm32f4` PAC gives you access to every register and bitfield for that STM32 series.
- **Hardware Abstraction Layers (HALs)**: On top of PACs, HALs provide safe APIs to initialize and use peripherals without having to manipulate raw bits manually. For example, `stm32f4xx-hal` or `rp2040-hal` provide convenient interfaces for working with GPIOs, timers, and communication peripherals.

Let's look at a brief but real use case to demonstrate the value of this ecosystem. Suppose you're writing firmware for a weather sensor node that communicates over I2C with a BME280 sensor, logs temperature to UART, and powers down periodically to conserve battery. In traditional C, you'd likely write device-specific register code, manage UART buffers manually, and carefully disable peripherals before sleep.

In embedded Rust, you could wire this up using the HAL:

```
let mut i2c = I2C::i2c1(
    dp.I2C1,
```

```
        (scl, sda),
        100.kHz(),
        clocks,
        &mut rcc.apb1,
    );

    let mut sensor = BME280::new_primary(i2c, delay);

    let temperature =
    sensor.read_temperature().unwrap();

    writeln!(uart, "Temperature: {}°C",
    temperature).unwrap();
```

This is production-level firmware using real hardware traits, safe abstractions, and composable logic. And under the hood, you're still getting tightly optimized assembly with zero dynamic overhead.

Tooling support has also matured significantly. The **probe-rs** project enables flashing and debugging microcontroller firmware using Rust-native tooling— no need to configure OpenOCD unless you want to. With `cargo-flash` and `cargo-embed`, you can build, upload, and trace your firmware from the same environment you write your code in.

In addition, **Real-Time Interrupt-driven Concurrency (RTIC)** is another important piece of the ecosystem. RTIC is a framework for writing concurrent embedded Rust applications without needing an RTOS. It handles interrupt scheduling, task priorities, and shared resource access in a way that guarantees memory safety and predictable execution. RTIC is already being used in commercial embedded projects where concurrency and timing are critical.

All of this means that you're not just adopting a language—you're stepping into an ecosystem that's ready for real embedded work. From peripheral drivers to industrial safety certifications, from IoT boards to mission-critical aerospace systems, Rust is proving itself as a serious tool for embedded development. And as the community grows and the tooling becomes more refined, it's only going to get easier and more rewarding to build fast, safe firmware that you can trust to run unsupervised in the field.

Chapter 2: Getting Started with Bare-Metal Rust

Getting started with bare-metal Rust means stepping into an environment where you control everything—from how memory is laid out, to how bits are set in peripheral registers. This is a sharp contrast to desktop development, where the operating system manages memory, interrupts, and I/O on your behalf. In bare-metal programming, you're the OS.

That might sound intimidating, but with Rust's tooling and community, it's actually quite approachable. In this chapter, you'll set up your environment from scratch, configure your first `no_std` project, and build a simple firmware that runs on a microcontroller. By the end, you'll have everything you need to start experimenting on real hardware.

Installing Rust and Toolchains

Before you can start building firmware with Rust, you need to install the right tools. Rust's ecosystem has matured to a point where embedded development is not only possible but productive and ergonomic, provided your toolchain is set up correctly. In this section, we'll walk through installing Rust itself, adding support for cross-compilation, and preparing the environment to target bare-metal microcontrollers—particularly ARM Cortex-M devices, which are commonly used in embedded projects.

The installation process should be done with attention to detail. Every component you install plays a critical role in the toolchain, and missing or misconfigured parts can lead to subtle issues when you're compiling or flashing code to real hardware.

Let's start with the installation of Rust.

Rust uses a tool called `rustup` to manage installations. `rustup` is the official way to install Rust and lets you easily switch between versions and targets. It also installs `cargo`, Rust's package manager and build system.

If you haven't already installed `rustup`, open a terminal and run:

```
curl --proto '=https' --tlsv1.2 -sSf
https://sh.rustup.rs | sh
```

This script downloads and installs the Rust toolchain along with `cargo`. After installation, ensure your terminal environment is up to date by restarting the shell or reloading your profile:

```
source $HOME/.cargo/env
```

Now verify that everything is installed correctly:

```
rustc --version
```

```
cargo --version
```

You should see output showing the current version of the compiler and Cargo. These tools are essential. You'll use `cargo` to compile your firmware, manage dependencies, and run custom commands during development.

Rust is designed to support multiple targets. On your desktop, the default target is usually `x86_64-unknown-linux-gnu` or a similar variant depending on your OS. But for embedded work, you'll be targeting microcontrollers— often with no operating system and very limited resources.

For bare-metal development on ARM Cortex-M processors, you need to add a cross-compilation target. This is typically something like `thumbv7em-none-eabihf`, which corresponds to Cortex-M4 and M7 devices with hardware floating-point support.

Add the target like this:

```
rustup target add thumbv7em-none-eabihf
```

This tells Rust to download and install the appropriate libraries for cross-compiling code to this target.

Next, you need a linker that understands how to produce binaries for ARM Cortex-M architectures. On most Linux distributions, you can install the required tools using your system package manager. If you're using Ubuntu or Debian, run:

```
sudo apt update
```

```
sudo apt install gcc-arm-none-eabi gdb-arm-none-
eabi
```

If you're on macOS and using Homebrew, the process looks like this:

```
brew tap ArmMbed/homebrew-formulae
```

```
brew install arm-none-eabi-gcc
```

Windows users can install the ARM toolchain via MSYS2, Scoop, or the official ARM website.

Let's confirm it's working:

```
arm-none-eabi-gcc --version
```

You should see a version message. This confirms that you can compile code for ARM microcontrollers. Later on, this toolchain will be used by `cargo` to link your final firmware binary correctly.

For debugging and flashing, Rust has native support for hardware debuggers through a tool called `probe-rs`. It works with many common debug probes like ST-Link, J-Link, and CMSIS-DAP, and it eliminates the need to manually configure `OpenOCD`.

Install `probe-rs` and its helpers:

```
cargo install probe-rs
cargo install cargo-flash
cargo install cargo-embed
```

These tools give you the ability to flash firmware, log debug output, and even interact with memory and registers while the device is running.

Let's summarize with a quick check. At this point, you should have:

- Rust compiler (`rustc`) and Cargo installed
- A cross-compilation target (`thumbv7em-none-eabihf`) added
- An ARM toolchain (`arm-none-eabi-gcc`) installed
- `probe-rs`, `cargo-flash`, and `cargo-embed` available for flashing and debugging

Try running this command:

```
cargo new bare-metal-check --bin
cd bare-metal-check
cargo build --target thumbv7em-none-eabihf
```

You'll get a linker error at this point—and that's expected. The compiler was able to target the architecture correctly, which means your setup is working. In the next section, you'll learn how to configure your project with a linker script, disable the standard library, and write your first working firmware.

This entire setup process, while technical, is foundational. Once it's in place, you'll have a repeatable toolchain that gives you full control over every instruction your microcontroller runs—without ever sacrificing safety or clarity. That's the value Rust brings to embedded development, and it starts right here.

Setting Up the Project Environment

Now that you have Rust and the necessary toolchains installed, the next step is setting up your project environment in a way that's tailored for embedded, bare-metal development. This isn't your usual Rust application. You won't be using the standard library, and you won't rely on an operating system to provide memory management or I/O. Your firmware will run directly on the metal—so you need to configure the project to behave accordingly.

Let's walk through creating and configuring a new embedded Rust project from scratch, using industry-standard conventions and tools that will carry you through real-world development.

Start by installing `cargo-generate`, a helpful tool that allows you to scaffold new Rust projects from predefined templates:

```
cargo install cargo-generate
```

Once installed, use it to generate a fresh embedded project based on the official template from the Rust Embedded Working Group:

```
cargo generate --git https://github.com/rust-embedded/cortex-m-quickstart.git --name bare-metal-project
```

```
cd bare-metal-project
```

This template gives you a functional starting point for ARM Cortex-M development. It includes a proper memory layout, a working build configuration, and the boilerplate needed to write a `no_std` firmware. It's been tested and refined by embedded Rust developers and is well-suited for real hardware experimentation.

Inside your new project, open the `Cargo.toml` file. You'll see standard metadata, but also some embedded-specific dependencies like:

```
[dependencies]
cortex-m = "0.7"
cortex-m-rt = "0.7"
panic-halt = "0.2"
```

The `cortex-m` crate provides core low-level ARM functionality, while `cortex-m-rt` sets up the runtime and interrupt vector table. The `panic-halt` crate defines what happens when the program panics—usually, it just freezes execution, which is safe behavior in embedded environments without an OS.

Let's look at `.cargo/config.toml`. This file tells Cargo which architecture to compile for:

```
[build]
target = "thumbv7em-none-eabihf"
```

With this configuration, all `cargo build` commands will produce binaries for Cortex-M4 and Cortex-M7 microcontrollers that support hardware floating-point. If you're working with a different chip—say, Cortex-M0 or a target without FPU—you'll use a different `thumbv*` target string here.

The heart of any embedded firmware project is the `src/main.rs` file. Open it and you'll see:

```
#![no_std]
#![no_main]

use cortex_m_rt::entry;

#[entry]
```

```
fn main() -> ! {
    loop {
        // your application logic goes here
    }
}
```

Two key attributes appear at the top:

- `#![no_std]` disables the Rust standard library.
- `#![no_main]` tells the compiler not to use the usual `fn main()` entry point. Instead, you'll define your own entry point using the `#[entry]` attribute provided by `cortex-m-rt`.

In a traditional desktop Rust application, you rely on the OS to initialize memory, set up the stack, and call your main function. In embedded Rust, that responsibility is passed to `cortex-m-rt`, which sets up the stack pointer, clears the `.bss` section, and then calls your `#[entry]` function.

Before your project can be linked into a working firmware binary, you need a linker script. This tells the linker where in memory to place various parts of your program—code, data, stack, and so on. The `memory.x` file in the root of your project provides this information.

Here's a sample content:

```
MEMORY
{
   FLASH : ORIGIN = 0x08000000, LENGTH = 512K
   RAM   : ORIGIN = 0x20000000, LENGTH = 128K
}
```

These memory addresses must match the specifications of your target microcontroller. For example, an STM32F401 has 512 KB of Flash starting at `0x08000000` and 96 KB of RAM starting at `0x20000000`. You'll need to adjust this file if you're working with a different chip.

To make sure your project uses this linker script during the build, open `.cargo/config.toml` and ensure it has a section like this:

```
[unstable]
build-std = ["core"]
```

```
[target.thumbv7em-none-eabihf]
runner = "probe-rs run"
rustflags = [
  "-C", "link-arg=-Tlink.x"
]
```

This setup specifies how to pass the linker script (link.x, which typically includes or aliases memory.x) to the build process and defines a runner command to flash and execute the firmware using probe-rs.

You also need to define a panic behavior. Since you're not using the standard library, there's no default panic handler. Choose one that matches your debugging and runtime needs. For development, panic-halt is a good starting point:

```
use panic_halt as _;
```

Later on, if you want to send panic messages over UART or log them through RTT, you can switch to panic-semihosting, panic-probe, or a custom panic handler that integrates with defmt.

At this point, you have a project that will compile, link, and run (provided you've connected supported hardware). To test this, try building the project:

```
cargo build --release
```

The output will be placed in target/thumbv7em-none-eabihf/release/bare-metal-project. This is a raw ELF binary that can be flashed directly to your microcontroller.

If you have your development board connected (e.g., an STM32 Nucleo or a micro:bit), and you've installed probe-rs, you can flash the binary using:

```
cargo flash --chip STM32F401RE --release
```

Replace STM32F401RE with the correct chip model for your board. If successful, your board will reset and begin executing the new firmware.

This setup—while low-level—forms the foundation of professional embedded Rust development. You've defined how memory is used, told Rust what target to build for, customized the runtime startup process, and created a firmware binary ready to run on physical hardware. Going forward, you'll build on this environment to interact with peripherals, handle interrupts, and develop reliable embedded applications with confidence and precision.

no_std, memory.x, and Target Specifications

When you're building bare-metal firmware in Rust, you're working without the conveniences of a host operating system. There are no threads, no heap, no system calls, no standard output. The environment is minimal—and that's exactly what makes embedded work powerful but demanding. To operate in this space, Rust must be told very clearly how to behave: what platform you're targeting, what memory it has, and what features are allowed.

This section will explain three foundational elements that every bare-metal Rust project needs to understand and configure correctly: the `no_std` attribute, the `memory.x` linker script, and the cross-compilation target specification.

Writing Rust Without the Standard Library (`no_std`)

By default, Rust applications include the standard library, which provides features like heap allocation, file I/O, and multithreading. In embedded systems, these features don't apply. Instead, you'll strip away the standard library and use only the `core` crate, which includes just the essentials—data types, math operations, formatting, and a few utilities.

To disable the standard library, your `main.rs` must begin with:

```
#![no_std]
```

This tells the compiler to skip linking against `std` and instead use `core`. You'll still have access to types like `Result`, `Option`, and `Iterator`, but you won't have things like `Vec`, `Box`, or `println!`. Those are tied to heap allocation and I/O, which don't exist on a bare-metal system unless you implement them yourself.

For example, here's a basic firmware stub with no standard library:

```
#![no_std]
#![no_main]
```

```rust
use cortex_m_rt::entry;

#[entry]
fn main() -> ! {
    loop {
        // Firmware logic goes here
    }
}
```

The `#![no_main]` attribute disables the default entry point. Instead, you provide a custom entry function using the `#[entry]` macro from `cortex-m-rt`. This function is where your firmware begins executing after the microcontroller resets and basic memory initialization is performed.

Defining Memory Layout with `memory.x`

Unlike a desktop system where the OS abstracts memory for you, in embedded systems you're responsible for specifying exactly where in physical memory your program lives. This is handled using a **linker script**. In Rust projects, it's often named `memory.x`.

The `memory.x` file defines two critical memory regions: **FLASH** and **RAM**. FLASH is where the program code and constant data are stored. RAM is where runtime data like the stack, heap (if used), and global/static variables reside.

Here's an example of a typical `memory.x` for an STM32F4 microcontroller:

```
MEMORY
{
  FLASH : ORIGIN = 0x08000000, LENGTH = 512K
  RAM   : ORIGIN = 0x20000000, LENGTH = 128K
}
```

These addresses must match your microcontroller's reference manual. If you're using a chip with only 64 KB of RAM or a different base address, you must update this script accordingly. An incorrect layout will either cause the program to fail silently or crash immediately after reset.

The `link.x` file (provided by `cortex-m-rt`) will include this `memory.x` file and use it during the linking phase to place `.text`, `.data`, `.bss`, `.stack`, and other sections correctly.

To ensure the linker sees this file, you need to configure Cargo to pass it along. In your `.cargo/config.toml`, add:

```
[target.thumbv7em-none-eabihf]
rustflags = ["-C", "link-arg=-Tlink.x"]
```

This line explicitly tells the compiler to use the custom linker script.

Configuring the Target Architecture

Rust is capable of targeting dozens of architectures, but your host platform (e.g., x86_64 Linux) is not the one you're programming firmware for. You need to compile code for your specific microcontroller architecture, such as ARM Cortex-M.

The target triple specifies the architecture, vendor, OS, and ABI (application binary interface). For example, the target triple `thumbv7em-none-eabihf` breaks down as follows:

- `thumbv7em`: the CPU architecture (Cortex-M4/M7)
- `none`: no operating system
- `eabihf`: embedded ABI with hardware floating-point support

To add this target to your Rust installation:

```
rustup target add thumbv7em-none-eabihf
```

Then, configure your project to build for this target by default. In `.cargo/config.toml`, add:

```
[build]
target = "thumbv7em-none-eabihf"
```

With this configuration in place, every time you run `cargo build`, the compiler produces a binary for the ARM Cortex-M architecture instead of your PC.

Here's an example `config.toml` in full:

```
[build]
target = "thumbv7em-none-eabihf"
```

```
[target.thumbv7em-none-eabihf]
runner = "probe-rs run"
rustflags = [
  "-C", "link-arg=-Tlink.x"
]
```

The `runner` specifies the tool used to run or flash the program. Here we use `probe-rs`, which automatically detects your hardware and writes the firmware.

Pulling It All Together

Let's put all these pieces into context with a working firmware skeleton:

```
#![no_std]
#![no_main]

use cortex_m_rt::entry;
use panic_halt as _; // halts on panic

#[entry]
fn main() -> ! {
    loop {
        // You could toggle a GPIO pin here
    }
}
```

With the correct `memory.x`, a target triple defined, and the build configuration in place, this binary can now be built and flashed to an ARM Cortex-M board.

Build the firmware:

```
cargo build --release
```

Flash it (assuming an STM32F4 chip):

```
cargo flash --chip STM32F401RE --release
```

If everything is configured correctly, your microcontroller will begin executing the code you've written—without an operating system, without standard library support, and with full control over every register and memory address.

This is the foundation of embedded Rust: precise, powerful, and predictable. When you define your memory layout, choose your target correctly, and write code in `no_std`, you're taking direct control of the machine, with the confidence that the compiler is helping you stay safe at every step.

Your First Minimal Firmware

Now that you've set up your embedded Rust environment, selected the correct target architecture, configured the memory layout, and built a `no_std` project, it's time to write your first actual firmware—the kind that can be flashed onto real hardware and verified with your own eyes. For this, we'll keep things very simple: a minimal firmware that toggles an LED in a loop. This gives you a working feedback loop from code to hardware, and it introduces key concepts like peripheral access and delay.

The goal here isn't to build a fancy application. It's to prove that everything is wired up correctly—from your Rust code, to the build system, to the physical microcontroller running your compiled binary.

Let's assume you're working with an ARM Cortex-M based board that has an onboard LED connected to a GPIO pin. Common examples include STM32 Nucleo boards, the micro:bit, and RP2040 boards.

Project Preparation

If you haven't done so already, add the appropriate hardware abstraction layer (HAL) to your `Cargo.toml`. For STM32F401RE (a common Nucleo board), add:

```
[dependencies]
cortex-m = "0.7"
cortex-m-rt = "0.7"
panic-halt = "0.2"
stm32f4xx-hal = { version = "0.16.0", features =
["stm32f401", "rt"] }
```

This tells Cargo to pull in the HAL with the right device-specific features. The `rt` feature ensures the runtime support (interrupt vector table, startup code) is linked in.

Writing the Firmware

Open `src/main.rs` and replace its contents with the following code:

```
#![no_std]
#![no_main]

use cortex_m_rt::entry;
use panic_halt as _;
use stm32f4xx_hal as hal;

use hal::prelude::*;
use hal::stm32;

#[entry]
fn main() -> ! {
    // Get access to the device-specific
peripherals
    let dp = stm32::Peripherals::take().unwrap();

    // Constrain and freeze the clock system
    let rcc = dp.RCC.constrain();
    let clocks = rcc.cfgr.freeze();

    // Split GPIO ports into independent pins
    let gpioc = dp.GPIOC.split();

    // Configure PC13 as a push-pull output
(onboard LED on Nucleo boards)
    let mut led =
gpioc.pc13.into_push_pull_output();

    // Blink loop
    loop {
        // Turn the LED on
        led.set_low().unwrap(); // On many boards,
low turns the LED on
        delay(clocks.sysclk().0 / 4);
```

```
        // Turn the LED off
        led.set_high().unwrap();
        delay(clocks.sysclk().0 / 4);
    }
}

// A simple busy-loop delay
fn delay(cycles: u32) {
    for _ in 0..cycles {
        cortex_m::asm::nop();
    }
}
```

Let's unpack what's happening here.

- The #![no_std] and #![no_main] attributes tell the compiler you're in bare-metal mode.
- #[entry] marks the main function as the firmware entry point. This is what gets executed after reset.
- Peripherals::take() safely provides access to the microcontroller's memory-mapped peripherals.
- The clock configuration is done via rcc.cfgr.freeze(), which sets up the system clock based on defaults or options.
- GPIO pin PC13 is configured as a digital output. This pin controls the onboard LED on most STM32 Nucleo boards.
- The loop toggles the LED with a crude delay function that burns cycles using nop() (no operation). This isn't power efficient, but it's predictable and sufficient for early testing.

Building the Firmware

Make sure your project is targeting the right architecture. Your .cargo/config.toml should look like this:

```
[build]
target = "thumbv7em-none-eabihf"

[target.thumbv7em-none-eabihf]
runner = "probe-rs run"
rustflags = ["-C", "link-arg=-Tlink.x"]
```

Now build the firmware:

```
cargo build --release
```

The compiled binary will be located at:

```
target/thumbv7em-none-eabihf/release/<your-project-
name>
```

You're ready to flash it.

Flashing the Firmware

Connect your development board to your computer via USB. If you're using an ST-Link debugger, J-Link, or a CMSIS-DAP probe, `probe-rs` should recognize it automatically.

Flash the binary using:

```
cargo flash --chip STM32F401RE --release
```

Replace `STM32F401RE` with the specific chip on your board if different. After a few seconds, your board will reboot and the LED should begin blinking at a regular interval.

If the LED doesn't blink, double-check the pin you're using, and make sure the board's reference manual maps that pin to an LED. You can also connect a logic analyzer or multimeter to the pin to check the voltage toggling.

This simple LED blinking firmware might seem trivial, but it's your first end-to-end confirmation that your Rust toolchain is working correctly for bare-metal embedded development. You've cross-compiled Rust code, linked it with a custom memory layout, and flashed it onto real hardware. You've also written firmware in a language that enforces memory safety, prevents race conditions, and produces highly efficient binaries—all without the crutches of an operating system.

From here, the path forward is clear. You can now build on this by introducing timers, interrupts, serial communication, and more complex peripheral interactions. But this LED blink is your foundation—it proves the whole toolchain is solid. Every firmware project you write in Rust will follow the same basic steps you've taken here, with this same level of clarity and safety baked in from the start.

Chapter 3: Exploring the `no_std` Environment

The world of embedded systems is built on precision and minimalism. In this space, every byte of memory matters and every cycle of execution needs to be accounted for. That's why, when working with Rust on bare-metal devices, you're going to be writing your firmware in an environment that doesn't use the standard library. This is what's known as the `no_std` environment.

The name might sound like a restriction, but it's really just a different context—one where you're closer to the hardware, and more in control. In this chapter, we'll explore what the `no_std` environment actually is, what Rust still offers you in this mode, how to handle runtime issues like panics, and what it really means to write code without a heap. By the end, you'll not only understand the technical reasons behind `no_std`, but you'll also feel at home inside it.

Rust Without the Standard Library

When writing firmware for a bare-metal microcontroller, there is no operating system, no file system, no heap allocator, and often no form of I/O except the ones you implement yourself. In this context, most of what the Rust standard library provides becomes irrelevant. That's why embedded Rust developers work in a mode called `no_std`—a version of Rust that omits the standard library entirely.

Working without the standard library may sound like a serious limitation at first, but it's not. It simply means you are telling Rust to operate in a smaller, more constrained environment. And Rust was designed to make this possible without giving up its safety, predictability, or expressiveness.

Why the Standard Library Is Not Included by Default in Embedded

Let's start with what the standard library (`std`) actually depends on. At its core, it assumes the presence of certain OS-level services. These include dynamic memory allocation via a system heap, system-level threading and synchronization, file and network I/O, error reporting via stderr, and the ability to cleanly terminate the process. In a microcontroller, none of these features are available unless you explicitly implement them yourself.

As a result, when targeting bare-metal systems, Rust needs to be told not to include `std`. This is done using the following crate-level attribute:

```
#![no_std]
```

Once this is in place, the compiler won't link the standard library. Instead, it links the `core` crate. This crate contains all the essentials you need to write software logic—without assuming you're running on an OS.

Here's what a minimal embedded Rust program looks like:

```
#![no_std]
#![no_main]

use cortex_m_rt::entry;

#[entry]
fn main() -> ! {
    loop {
        // your logic here
    }
}
```

This is the correct way to start firmware for a bare-metal target like an STM32, RP2040, or nRF52. You disable the standard runtime, and you define your own entry point using the `#[entry]` macro provided by `cortex-m-rt`. This is where execution begins after the chip resets.

What You Still Get With `no_std`

The `core` crate forms the foundation of `std`. It is always available in every Rust environment, and when you opt out of the standard library, `core` becomes your base toolkit.

It gives you:

- **Primitives** like `i32`, `f64`, `bool`, and `char`
- **Collections-like types** such as arrays, slices, and fixed-size tuples
- **Enums** such as `Option<T>` and `Result<T, E>` for safe error handling

- **Traits** including `Copy`, `Clone`, `Debug`, `Eq`, `PartialOrd`, and `Iterator`
- **Modules** like `core::mem`, `core::cmp`, and `core::ops`

These tools allow you to write expressive, maintainable, and efficient embedded logic. For example, you can pattern match on `Option<T>` to handle nullability without writing manual null checks. You can build iterator-based code to manipulate slices without using the heap.

Here's a simple example that reads values from a sensor array and finds the maximum:

```
fn max_sample(samples: &[u16]) -> u16 {
    *samples.iter().max().unwrap_or(&0)
}
```

This kind of high-level expression is fully supported in `no_std`. There's no heap here, no threads, and no OS—just safe, statically verified code compiled into a binary that runs on bare silicon.

What You Lose (And Don't Really Need)

What you don't get in `no_std` is anything that would normally require OS support:

- No `Vec`, `String`, or dynamic containers (unless you add the `alloc` crate)
- No threads, mutexes, or channels
- No `println!` or file operations
- No panic messages printed to a console
- No heap unless you explicitly provide a global allocator

But most of these are not needed in embedded work. You won't be opening files from disk. You won't be launching threads. You won't need dynamically resizing data structures if you know your memory constraints and allocate appropriately ahead of time.

What you do instead is work with static or stack-allocated data. This gives you tight control over memory usage and deterministic performance. You define buffers at compile time, manage data lifetimes explicitly, and use synchronization primitives like interrupt-free critical sections where necessary.

Here's a fixed-size ring buffer example using an array:

```rust
struct RingBuffer {
    data: [u8; 64],
    head: usize,
    tail: usize,
}

impl RingBuffer {
    fn new() -> Self {
        Self { data: [0; 64], head: 0, tail: 0 }
    }

    fn push(&mut self, byte: u8) -> bool {
        let next = (self.head + 1) %
self.data.len();
        if next == self.tail {
            return false; // buffer full
        }
        self.data[self.head] = byte;
        self.head = next;
        true
    }

    fn pop(&mut self) -> Option<u8> {
        if self.head == self.tail {
            return None; // buffer empty
        }
        let byte = self.data[self.tail];
        self.tail = (self.tail + 1) %
self.data.len();
        Some(byte)
    }
}
```

This ring buffer does not require heap allocation. It works entirely in `no_std`, and is appropriate for UART or SPI data buffering in microcontrollers.

How This Affects Your Project Structure

Once you declare `#![no_std]`, your development workflow needs to include a few additional components:

- A **runtime crate** like `cortex-m-rt` for ARM Cortex-M devices. This provides the interrupt vector table, stack setup, and entry point glue code.
- A **panic handler**, which defines what the program should do when a `panic!()` occurs. A common crate is `panic-halt`, which just stops execution.
- A **linker script**, which defines where in memory your code and data live. This is usually named `memory.x` and placed in the project root.
- A **target specification**, telling Cargo which architecture to build for (e.g., `thumbv7em-none-eabihf`).

Once these are configured, you're no longer writing a Rust application—you're writing firmware. And it behaves like one: it links to raw memory, runs without an OS, and executes deterministically.

Working without the standard library isn't limiting—it's liberating. It forces you to be precise, efficient, and aware of what your code is doing at the lowest level. And Rust gives you the tools to do that with confidence, without the usual risks of memory corruption or undefined behavior.

The `core` and `alloc` Crates

In embedded Rust development, when you opt out of the standard library using `#![no_std]`, you don't lose access to Rust's foundational capabilities. What actually happens is that your project continues to depend on two smaller, purpose-built crates: `core` and, optionally, `alloc`. These crates provide essential functionality for writing expressive, efficient, and safe code without relying on operating system features.

The `core` Crate: The Foundation of `no_std`

The `core` crate is always available in Rust, regardless of whether you're using `std`. It provides the most fundamental building blocks of the language—types, traits, macros, and functions that require no heap allocation, no threads, and no OS.

You don't have to explicitly write `extern crate core;`—Rust automatically links `core` when `#![no_std]` is in effect.

Here's what `core` gives you access to:

- Scalar types like `u8`, `u32`, `i64`, `bool`, and `char`
- Tuples, arrays, and slices
- Common enums like `Option<T>` and `Result<T, E>`
- Traits like `Copy`, `Clone`, `Eq`, `Ord`, `Default`, `Iterator`
- Functional combinators like `.map()`, `.filter()`, and `.fold()`
- Modules like `core::mem`, `core::ptr`, `core::cmp`, `core::ops`

These are all things you'll rely on heavily when writing firmware logic. For example, pattern matching with `Option<T>` is a clean, safe alternative to null pointers:

```
fn find_max(data: &[u32]) -> Option<u32> {
    data.iter().copied().max()
}
```

Or, you can write safe fallbacks using `Result<T, E>`:

```
fn read_temperature(raw: u16) -> Result<f32,
&'static str> {
    if raw == 0 {
        Err("Sensor disconnected")
    } else {
        Ok((raw as f32) * 0.1)
    }
}
```

These constructs are fully available in `no_std` through `core`, and the compiler applies all its usual type checks and optimizations.

Another essential feature of `core` is its support for zero-cost abstractions. Traits like `Iterator` and `IntoIterator` let you write functional-style code that is transformed at compile time into highly efficient loops—without dynamic dispatch or runtime cost.

Here's an example of a checksum computation using a slice and iterators:

```
fn compute_checksum(data: &[u8]) -> u8 {
    data.iter().fold(0u8, |acc, &b|
acc.wrapping_add(b))
}
```

This code compiles into a tight loop without any heap usage, pointer arithmetic, or unsafe blocks. It's readable, correct, and extremely efficient.

The `alloc` Crate: Opting into Dynamic Memory

While `core` gives you a powerful base, it doesn't provide dynamic memory allocation. That means types like `Vec`, `String`, `Box`, and `Rc` are unavailable in pure `no_std`. If you need dynamic containers or runtime flexibility, you can explicitly opt into the `alloc` crate.

To do that, your project needs:

1. An explicit dependency on `alloc`
2. A global memory allocator defined with `#[global_allocator]`
3. A hardware platform with a memory region that can be used as a heap

Here's how you enable `alloc` in your `Cargo.toml`:

```
[dependencies]
alloc = { version = "1.0", default-features = false
}
linked_list_allocator = "0.9"
```

In `main.rs` (or `lib.rs`), you'd then declare:

```
#![no_std]
extern crate alloc;

use alloc::vec::Vec;
use linked_list_allocator::LockedHeap;

#[global_allocator]
static ALLOCATOR: LockedHeap = LockedHeap::empty();

#[entry]
fn main() -> ! {
    use core::mem::MaybeUninit;

    static mut HEAP: MaybeUninit<[u8; 1024]> =
MaybeUninit::uninit();

    unsafe {
```

```
        ALLOCATOR.lock().init(HEAP.as_mut_ptr() as
usize, 1024);
    }

    let mut numbers = Vec::new();
    numbers.push(1);
    numbers.push(2);
    numbers.push(3);

    loop {}
}
```

In this example, we:

- Enable the `alloc` crate.
- Define a 1 KB heap using a static buffer.
- Initialize the allocator during runtime setup.
- Use a `Vec` to store values dynamically.

This works in environments where you control the memory layout, and where allocation patterns are predictable and bounded.

But it comes with trade-offs. Using dynamic allocation increases your firmware's complexity and introduces the potential for fragmentation. It's harder to reason about in real-time or safety-critical systems. That's why many embedded Rust projects avoid `alloc` unless there's a clear need for it—such as buffering variable-length network packets or supporting pluggable configuration structures.

When to Use `core` Alone vs. Add `alloc`

Most embedded firmware projects will never need `alloc`. They deal with fixed-size buffers, preallocated data, and stack-local structures. For these, `core` is more than sufficient.

Use `alloc` when:

- You need runtime flexibility in data size or shape
- You're implementing features like heap-allocated queues or resizable buffers
- You're working with a platform that has significant free RAM and no strict real-time constraints

45

Stick to `core` when:

- You're targeting real-time or safety-critical systems
- Your memory usage needs to be strictly bounded and predictable
- You're operating with very limited RAM (e.g., < 16 KB)

In either case, Rust lets you make that decision explicitly and locally. You're never forced to bring in the full standard library, and you can even mix static and dynamic strategies safely.

The `core` and `alloc` crates form the backbone of embedded Rust development. One gives you everything you need to build safe, efficient firmware without any dynamic memory. The other, when explicitly chosen and configured, opens the door to more flexible design patterns. And because both are tightly integrated with Rust's ownership and type systems, you don't sacrifice safety or clarity—no matter which path you take.

Panic Handlers and Error Hooks

In a desktop or server application, when something goes wrong—such as an out-of-bounds array access, a failed assertion, or an unwrapped `None`—Rust responds with a panic. By default, it prints a helpful message, points to the exact line of code, and either aborts or unwinds the stack depending on your build profile. But in an embedded system, there's no terminal to print to, no standard output, and no operating system to cleanly recover or log crash reports.

In `no_std` environments, panics are a different beast. If you don't handle them explicitly, your firmware won't even compile. That's because in bare-metal Rust, you must define what happens when a panic occurs. This is done through *panic handlers*.

What Happens When a Panic Occurs

When Rust encounters a problem at runtime that it can't recover from—like unwrapping a `None`, calling `expect()` and failing, or manually invoking `panic!()`—it calls a special function known as the **panic handler**.

In `no_std`, you are responsible for providing that function. If you don't, the linker will complain that the symbol `rust_begin_unwind` is undefined. That's your cue to implement a custom handler.

A panic handler is defined like this:

```
use core::panic::PanicInfo;

#[panic_handler]
fn panic(info: &PanicInfo) -> ! {
    loop {}
}
```

The `PanicInfo` struct contains information about what caused the panic—most usefully, the file and line number if available. But in `no_std`, this information is limited unless you also configure debugging support (which we'll cover shortly).

The return type is `!`, pronounced "never". It tells the compiler that this function will never return. That's important because if the panic handler returned control back to the main loop, you could end up with undefined behavior.

In many embedded applications, the goal of the panic handler is simple: stop the processor and wait for a watchdog reset. Sometimes developers also use the panic to blink an LED in a specific pattern or output a debug message over serial.

Here's a practical version:

```
use core::panic::PanicInfo;
use cortex_m::asm;

#[panic_handler]
fn panic(_info: &PanicInfo) -> ! {
    // Optionally log info to UART or LED here
    loop {
        asm::bkpt(); // trigger a breakpoint for
debugger
    }
}
```

In this version, the `bkpt` instruction creates a breakpoint trap. If you're connected to a debugger, it will pause execution here—letting you inspect registers and memory to figure out what went wrong.

Using Existing Panic Implementations

For convenience, the Rust ecosystem offers several panic crates you can plug in depending on your debugging setup.

```
panic-halt
```

The simplest option. When a panic occurs, the system halts by entering an infinite loop.

```
# Cargo.toml
[dependencies]
panic-halt = "0.2"
use panic_halt as _;
panic-semihosting
```

This prints the panic message over a semihosted I/O channel, assuming you are debugging with OpenOCD or a J-Link:

```
panic-semihosting = "0.5"
use panic_semihosting as _;
```

Now, if your code panics, you'll see a message like:

```
panicked at 'assertion failed: x == 42',
src/main.rs:12:9
```

in your debugger's output window.

panic-probe with defmt

If you're using `defmt`, the embedded logging framework, `panic-probe` allows the panic message to be output via RTT:

```
[dependencies]
defmt = "0.3"
defmt-rtt = "0.4"
panic-probe = "0.3"
use defmt_rtt as _;
use panic_probe as _;
```

This integrates nicely with `cargo-embed` and displays structured logs in your terminal.

Customizing Panic Behavior

You can write your own panic handler if the existing ones don't fit your needs. For instance, you may want to light an LED, reset peripherals, or reboot the system:

```
#[panic_handler]
fn panic(_info: &PanicInfo) -> ! {
    unsafe {
        let gpio = &*stm32::GPIOC::ptr();
        gpio.odr.modify(|_, w|
w.odr13().set_bit()); // Turn on PC13 LED
    }

    loop {}
}
```

Here, a panic turns on an onboard LED. This works even without a debugger and gives immediate feedback when something goes wrong.

Panic in Debug vs. Release Builds

By default, Rust uses two different panic strategies depending on your build profile:

- **Debug mode (`cargo build`)** uses `panic = "unwind"` unless overridden.
- **Release mode (`cargo build --release`)** uses `panic = "abort"`.

In embedded development, you should always use `panic = "abort"` because unwinding requires heap structures and exception metadata that aren't available in `no_std`. You can enforce this in your Cargo configuration:

```
[profile.dev]
panic = "abort"

[profile.release]
panic = "abort"
```

Error Hooks in `no_std`

Beyond panic handlers, you can also define **error hooks** for other failure types—though in bare-metal systems, these are rare. One area where error hooks are useful is when using `Result`-returning functions from core drivers or libraries and logging failures when they occur.

For example, in an embedded network stack, you might register an error handler that logs packet parsing failures or transport errors.

Most `no_std` code avoids fancy error dispatching for simplicity and determinism, but if your application needs it, Rust's trait system and type system can support it with structured error types, enums, and even inline fallbacks.

Handling panics explicitly is a normal part of embedded firmware development. Whether you halt, blink an LED, log over UART, or trigger a system reset, Rust gives you full control over what happens when something goes wrong. And because panic behavior is always defined at compile time in `no_std`, you're never guessing about what your firmware might do—it's entirely up to you, by design.

Working Without a Heap

In many embedded systems, dynamic memory allocation is not just discouraged—it's deliberately excluded. This is often due to a combination of reasons: predictability, memory limits, real-time constraints, and the desire for fail-safe operation. When you're working in a `no_std` Rust environment, there's no global allocator by default. That means types like `Vec`, `Box`, and `String` simply aren't available—unless you explicitly bring in the `alloc` crate and set up an allocator, which most production-grade firmware avoids.

Using Stack-Allocated Memory

Stack memory is the simplest and fastest kind of allocation in embedded programming. The processor handles it automatically. When a function is called, local variables are placed on the stack. When the function returns, those variables are removed. It's fast, efficient, and entirely deterministic.

Here's an example of using stack-allocated arrays in Rust:

```
fn average(values: &[u16]) -> u16 {
```

```
    let sum: u32 = values.iter().map(|&v| v as
u32).sum();
    (sum / values.len() as u32) as u16
}

#[entry]
fn main() -> ! {
    let data = [10, 20, 30, 40];
    let avg = average(&data);

    loop {}
}
```

Here, `data` is allocated on the stack. It's passed by reference as a slice to the `average` function, which iterates over it using Rust's zero-cost abstraction features.

Rust ensures that memory used by `data` is valid, bounds-checked, and never accessed after it goes out of scope. This eliminates a whole class of common bugs such as buffer overflows or use-after-free.

However, the stack is limited. Depending on the microcontroller, it might be as small as 1 KB to 8 KB. If you allocate large structures on the stack, you can cause a stack overflow, which in embedded systems often leads to a reset or undefined behavior.

Always be aware of your stack usage, especially in deeply nested or recursive code.

Using Statically Allocated Memory

When data needs to persist for the entire lifetime of the program, or when it must be shared across interrupt contexts, the best choice is **static memory**.

Rust allows you to define statics like this:

```
static mut COUNTER: u32 = 0;
```

However, static mut is **unsafe** to use directly because it can lead to data races if accessed from multiple contexts without synchronization.

You can access static mut variables like this:

```
unsafe {
    COUNTER += 1;
}
```

To avoid undefined behavior, you must ensure that this access is safe—typically by only reading or writing from one context at a time, or by wrapping access in a critical section.

A safer alternative is to use a `Mutex` with `RefCell`, especially in environments that support interrupts:

```
use cortex_m::interrupt::{self, Mutex};
use core::cell::RefCell;

static SHARED_DATA: Mutex<RefCell<Option<u8>>> =
Mutex::new(RefCell::new(None));

#[interrupt]
fn TIM2() {
    interrupt::free(|cs| {
        *SHARED_DATA.borrow(cs).borrow_mut() =
Some(42);
    });
}
```

This pattern guarantees memory safety while still working without dynamic allocation. The `Mutex` ensures safe access, while the `RefCell` gives interior mutability.

Fixed-Size Buffers as Alternatives to `Vec`

When you can't use `Vec`, you can use fixed-size arrays or libraries that provide capacity-limited containers.

Here's a hand-written example of a ring buffer:

```
struct RingBuffer {
    buffer: [u8; 64],
    head: usize,
    tail: usize,
}
```

```
impl RingBuffer {
    fn new() -> Self {
        Self {
            buffer: [0; 64],
            head: 0,
            tail: 0,
        }
    }

    fn push(&mut self, byte: u8) -> bool {
        let next = (self.head + 1) %
self.buffer.len();
        if next == self.tail {
            return false; // Buffer is full
        }
        self.buffer[self.head] = byte;
        self.head = next;
        true
    }

    fn pop(&mut self) -> Option<u8> {
        if self.head == self.tail {
            return None; // Buffer is empty
        }
        let byte = self.buffer[self.tail];
        self.tail = (self.tail + 1) %
self.buffer.len();
        Some(byte)
    }
}
```

This gives you the flexibility of a queue without needing heap allocation. It's especially useful for UART reception, sensor buffers, or any stream-oriented interface.

For more complex needs, the `heapless` crate provides efficient, no_std-compatible data structures that work with fixed capacity:

```
[dependencies]
heapless = "0.7"
use heapless::spsc::Queue;
```

```
static mut Q: Queue<u8, 8> = Queue::new();
```

This crate gives you `Vec`, `String`, maps, queues, and ring buffers that work entirely on preallocated memory. It's battle-tested and widely used in production firmware.

Design Patterns That Work Without a Heap

Working without dynamic allocation pushes you to structure your application differently—but in many ways, this leads to cleaner designs.

Use compile-time constants to define sizes:

```
const MAX_DEVICES: usize = 8;
let mut devices: [Device; MAX_DEVICES] =
[Device::default(); MAX_DEVICES];
```

Use enums with data-carrying variants to avoid dynamic polymorphism:

```
enum Command {
    Start,
    Stop,
    Write(u8),
}
```

Use slices to pass variable-length data without heap:

```
fn process(data: &[u8]) {
    for byte in data {
        // Do something
    }
}
```

Design APIs to work on borrowed buffers instead of returning owned data:

```
fn fill_buffer(buf: &mut [u8]) -> usize {
    buf[0] = 0xAB;
    1 // bytes written
}
```

These patterns all work without a heap, and they allow you to write zero-allocation code that is fast, safe, and portable.

54

Writing firmware without a heap is not a constraint—it's a principle. It forces discipline. It eliminates non-determinism. It gives you complete control over memory layout and usage. And with Rust's expressive type system, rich `core` functionality, and crates like `heapless`, you'll find that you rarely need to allocate dynamically in the first place.

Whether you're building for a 32 KB Cortex-M0 or a 512 KB Cortex-M4, writing heapless Rust code means your firmware stays small, reliable, and understandable—right from power-on to production.

Chapter 4: GPIO and Timing Control

Controlling hardware is one of the core tasks of embedded programming. Whether you're toggling an LED, driving a relay, or communicating with a peripheral device, you're doing it by reading from and writing to physical memory addresses that correspond to registers inside a microcontroller. This is called *memory-mapped I/O*, and it's the foundation of how Rust interacts with microcontroller peripherals.

In this chapter, you'll learn how to use memory-mapped I/O safely in Rust, how to access and control GPIO (General-Purpose Input/Output) pins, how to structure that access using Peripheral Access Crates (PACs) and Hardware Abstraction Layers (HALs), and how to create accurate delays using the system timer (SysTick). By the end, you'll understand how to interface with the outside world and schedule behavior with precise timing—without depending on an operating system.

Memory-Mapped I/O and Peripheral Access

At the hardware level, everything in an embedded system comes down to controlling and observing voltages on physical pins, reading data from memory-mapped registers, and writing values to those registers to drive behavior. This mechanism—known as **memory-mapped I/O**—is how microcontrollers expose peripheral features like GPIO, timers, UART, ADCs, and more to your code.

When you interact with a GPIO pin to turn an LED on or read a button press, you're not calling a function in the traditional sense—you're modifying specific bits at fixed memory addresses that correspond to control registers defined by the microcontroller's architecture.

In Rust, interacting with memory-mapped I/O is done safely and systematically using both low-level and high-level tools. But to truly appreciate how this works, it's important to understand the underlying concepts and how Rust's system programming capabilities are applied to hardware register access.

Microcontrollers map peripheral registers into a specific range of the system's address space. Reading or writing to an address in this range directly affects hardware.

For example, on many STM32 devices, the address `0x4800_0814` corresponds to the output data register for GPIO port C. Writing to this register updates the state of the physical output pins associated with GPIOC.

So if you write a `1` to bit 13 of this register, and if PC13 is configured as a push-pull output, it will drive that pin high—which might turn an LED off or on, depending on the circuit design.

Direct Register Access in Rust (Unsafe)

You can access this memory directly using raw pointers. This is inherently unsafe because the compiler can't guarantee correctness or side-effect safety when dealing with raw addresses.

Here's a basic example:

```rust
const GPIOC_ODR: *mut u32 = 0x48000814 as *mut u32;

fn set_led_on() {
    unsafe {
        let current =
core::ptr::read_volatile(GPIOC_ODR);
        core::ptr::write_volatile(GPIOC_ODR,
current | (1 << 13));
    }
}

fn set_led_off() {
    unsafe {
        let current =
core::ptr::read_volatile(GPIOC_ODR);
        core::ptr::write_volatile(GPIOC_ODR,
current & !(1 << 13));
    }
}
```

This code:

- Defines a pointer to the Output Data Register (ODR) of GPIOC
- Reads the current value using `read_volatile`
- Sets or clears bit 13 to control the LED
- Writes the result back using `write_volatile`

These operations are marked `unsafe` because they interact directly with memory outside Rust's control. If the address is wrong or the peripheral hasn't been enabled, your program could behave unpredictably or hang.

In production code, you want more structure and safety—without sacrificing low-level control.

Safer Peripheral Access with PACs (Peripheral Access Crates)

To manage complexity and provide safety, the Rust embedded ecosystem uses **PACs**, which are automatically generated from vendor-supplied SVD files. These crates give you access to every register and bitfield of the target microcontroller in a type-safe and documented way.

Here's how the same GPIO control would look using the `stm32f4` PAC:

```
use stm32f4::stm32f401;

fn toggle_led() {
    let dp =
stm32f401::Peripherals::take().unwrap();
    let gpioc = &dp.GPIOC;

    // Set pin PC13 to output
    gpioc.moder.modify(|_, w|
w.moder13().output());

    // Toggle PC13
    gpioc.odr.modify(|r, w|
w.odr13().bit(!r.odr13().bit()));
}
```

In this version:

- `Peripherals::take()` gives you exclusive access to all device peripherals.
- The `GPIOC` struct gives structured access to GPIO port C.

58

- `moder.modify()` changes the mode register, setting PC13 as an output.
- `odr.modify()` safely toggles the output state of the pin.

All of this is safe. You can't write to undefined bits. You can't write to peripherals that aren't enabled. And everything is expressed in terms of register fields rather than raw bit shifts and addresses.

Each field has semantic meaning. For example, `.moder13().output()` is clearer and safer than manually writing `0b01` to bits 27–26.

Practical Example: Setting Up GPIO with a PAC

Suppose you want to configure a GPIO pin and toggle it in a loop. Using the `stm32f4` PAC, this would look like:

```
#[entry]
fn main() -> ! {
    let dp =
stm32f401::Peripherals::take().unwrap();

    // Enable the GPIOC clock
    dp.RCC.ahb1enr.modify(|_, w|
w.gpiocen().set_bit());

    // Set PC13 to output
    dp.GPIOC.moder.modify(|_, w|
w.moder13().output());

    loop {
        // Toggle PC13
        dp.GPIOC.odr.modify(|r, w|
w.odr13().bit(!r.odr13().bit()));
        delay(); // crude busy-wait delay
    }
}

fn delay() {
    for _ in 0..1_000_000 {

core::sync::atomic::compiler_fence(core::sync::atom
ic::Ordering::SeqCst);
```

```
        }
    }
}
```

This program does three things:

1. Enables the peripheral clock for GPIOC.
2. Configures PC13 as a digital output.
3. Enters a loop where it toggles the pin and waits.

The `compiler_fence` prevents the compiler from optimizing away the delay loop, maintaining timing consistency across builds.

When and Why to Use Direct Access vs. PACs

Direct access using `unsafe` is useful when:

-   You're working with extremely low-level routines (bootloaders, minimal HALs)
-   You're building abstractions or libraries that must avoid dependencies
-   You need fine-tuned control and are comfortable taking responsibility for correctness

PACs are preferred when:

-   You want safety, readability, and maintainability
-   You need access to many different peripherals without memorizing register maps
-   You want to take advantage of compile-time checks for peripheral setup

In both cases, Rust gives you the choice. The key difference is that with PACs, many categories of bugs are eliminated at compile time, and you can focus on behavior rather than register trivia.

Understanding memory-mapped I/O is the core skill of embedded development. It's how you bridge software with hardware, and in Rust, you get the power to do it safely. Whether you're writing one-off experiments with raw pointers or building long-term production code using PACs, the control is yours—and it's backed by the confidence of strong types and compile-time validation.

Using PACs and HALs

When programming microcontrollers in Rust, you rarely want to rely on raw memory addresses and manual bit-twiddling in the long term—even if you start that way when learning. While using `unsafe` with volatile reads and writes is sometimes necessary, it's fragile, repetitive, and error-prone. The good news is that the Rust embedded ecosystem provides a structured, type-safe alternative: **Peripheral Access Crates (PACs)** and **Hardware Abstraction Layers (HALs)**.

What Is a PAC?

A **Peripheral Access Crate** is a device-specific Rust crate that gives you complete, low-level access to all the microcontroller's registers—every peripheral, every bitfield, every interrupt, all with type safety. These crates are auto-generated from **SVD (System View Description)** files using a tool called `svd2rust`.

SVD files are published by chip manufacturers like STMicroelectronics, Nordic, or NXP. They describe the structure of a microcontroller in XML—memory-mapped register layouts, peripheral names, field access types, and so on. `svd2rust` parses this data and emits a crate where each peripheral is a module, each register is a struct, and each bitfield is a method.

So with a PAC, instead of doing this:

```
const GPIOC_MODER: *mut u32 = 0x48000800 as *mut
u32;
unsafe {
    core::ptr::write_volatile(GPIOC_MODER,
0x00004000);
}
```

You can do this:

```
use stm32f4::stm32f401;

let dp = stm32f401::Peripherals::take().unwrap();
dp.GPIOC.moder.modify(|_, w| w.moder13().output());
```

You get full control, but with structure, autocomplete, and compile-time validation. PACs don't abstract anything—they expose the exact hardware capabilities, but with type safety and documentation. Every PAC crate maps one-to-one with the device's reference manual.

What Is a HAL?

A **Hardware Abstraction Layer** sits one level above a PAC. Instead of exposing every register, a HAL gives you an ergonomic, high-level API for interacting with common peripherals—GPIO, timers, I2C, SPI, ADC, UART, and so on.

HALs are built using the underlying PAC. They call PAC methods behind the scenes, but present a clean interface to your code.

Let's compare the PAC and HAL approaches to toggling an LED.

PAC-only GPIO (STM32F4):

```
let dp = stm32f401::Peripherals::take().unwrap();
dp.RCC.ahb1enr.modify(|_, w|
w.gpiocen().enabled());
dp.GPIOC.moder.modify(|_, w| w.moder13().output());
dp.GPIOC.odr.modify(|r, w|
w.odr13().bit(!r.odr13().bit()));
```

HAL-based GPIO (STM32F4xx-HAL):

```
use stm32f4xx_hal::prelude::*;
use stm32f4xx_hal::stm32;

let dp = stm32::Peripherals::take().unwrap();
let gpioc = dp.GPIOC.split();
let mut led = gpioc.pc13.into_push_pull_output();

led.set_high().unwrap(); // turns the LED off or on
depending on circuit
```

In the HAL version:

- You don't need to manually enable the GPIO peripheral clock
- You don't need to configure pin modes using raw bits

- You get concrete types that represent the pin's mode (e.g., output)
- You get trait-based methods (`set_high()`, `set_low()`, `toggle()`) with proper error handling

Under the hood, the HAL still calls the PAC. It's not hiding hardware—it's organizing it.

Real-World Example: Toggling an LED with the HAL

Here's a complete example using `stm32f4xx-hal` to blink an LED on a Nucleo board:

```rust
#![no_std]
#![no_main]

use cortex_m_rt::entry;
use panic_halt as _;
use stm32f4xx_hal::{
    pac,
    prelude::*,
    delay::Delay,
};

#[entry]
fn main() -> ! {
    let dp = pac::Peripherals::take().unwrap();
    let cp =
cortex_m::Peripherals::take().unwrap();

    let rcc = dp.RCC.constrain();
    let clocks = rcc.cfgr.freeze();

    let gpioc = dp.GPIOC.split();
    let mut led =
gpioc.pc13.into_push_pull_output();

    let mut delay = Delay::new(cp.SYST, clocks);

    loop {
        led.set_low().unwrap(); // LED on
        delay.delay_ms(250u32);
```

```
        led.set_high().unwrap();  // LED off
        delay.delay_ms(250u32);
    }
}
```

This uses the HAL's:

- Clock configuration tools
- GPIO pin struct and mode conversion
- Delay implementation built on SysTick

It's concise, type-safe, and production-ready.

Choosing When to Use PAC vs HAL

Use PACs when:

- You need precise control over registers or undocumented behavior
- You're writing a custom driver for a peripheral not supported by the HAL
- You want to implement your own abstraction or wrapper

Use HALs when:

- You want to write portable, readable firmware
- You need a quick way to interact with common peripherals
- You want to avoid touching register bits unless necessary

In many applications, you'll use both. Start with HALs for clean initialization and high-level tasks, and drop down to PACs when needed—just like you'd use safe Rust but drop into `unsafe` blocks for performance or control.

PACs and HALs are two of the best things about embedded Rust. They give you power and structure. They help you avoid the risks of pointer arithmetic and bit masking without sacrificing performance. And they make your firmware code clearer, safer, and easier to port to new chips.

Whether you're initializing clocks, configuring timers, or toggling GPIOs, using these tools means you're writing better firmware—not by hiding the hardware, but by organizing it. In the chapters ahead, you'll see how these same principles apply as we begin to handle timers, interrupts, and real-time events.

Blinking LEDs the Bare-Metal Way

There's a certain clarity that comes with writing bare-metal firmware. No operating system, no background services—just your code running directly on the hardware. When you control an LED from that level, you're not calling an API or using a convenience layer. You're writing values into specific memory addresses to manipulate pins on a microcontroller. This is fundamental embedded development, and in Rust, you can do it safely and with precision.

In this section, we'll build a minimal example that blinks an LED using direct register access—no HAL, no abstraction layers, just memory-mapped I/O. The goal is to show you how things work underneath the PACs and HALs, so that when you use higher-level libraries, you understand the mechanics they're built on. And when needed, you'll know exactly how to drop down to bare metal.

Choosing the Platform

Let's use the STM32F401 as our example platform, a common choice found on Nucleo boards. This microcontroller includes several GPIO ports, and PC13 is typically connected to the onboard user LED. If you're working with another board, adjust the GPIO port and pin as needed.

To blink the LED, we'll do four things:

1. Enable the clock for GPIOC.
2. Set PC13 as a push-pull output.
3. Toggle PC13 in a loop.
4. Insert a delay to make the blinking visible.

We'll write this using raw memory-mapped addresses and no_std Rust.

Full Example: LED Blinking With Bare-Metal Access

```
#![no_std]
#![no_main]

use cortex_m_rt::entry;
use cortex_m::asm;
use panic_halt as _;
```

```rust
// Constants for GPIOC base and register offsets
const RCC_AHB1ENR: *mut u32 = 0x4002_3830 as *mut
u32;
const GPIOC_MODER: *mut u32 = 0x4800_0800 as *mut
u32;
const GPIOC_ODR: *mut u32 = 0x4800_0814 as *mut
u32;

#[entry]
fn main() -> ! {
    // 1. Enable GPIOC clock
    unsafe {
        let rcc_en =
core::ptr::read_volatile(RCC_AHB1ENR);
        core::ptr::write_volatile(RCC_AHB1ENR,
rcc_en | (1 << 2)); // Bit 2 enables GPIOC
    }

    // 2. Set PC13 to output (bits 26:27 = 01)
    unsafe {
        let moder =
core::ptr::read_volatile(GPIOC_MODER);
        let cleared = moder & !(0b11 << 26);      //
Clear bits 26 and 27
        let set_output = cleared | (0b01 << 26); //
Set bit 26 to 1 (output)
        core::ptr::write_volatile(GPIOC_MODER,
set_output);
    }

    loop {
        // 3. Turn LED on (clear PC13)
        unsafe {
            let odr =
core::ptr::read_volatile(GPIOC_ODR);
            core::ptr::write_volatile(GPIOC_ODR,
odr & !(1 << 13));
        }

        delay(8_000_000); // crude delay

        // 4. Turn LED off (set PC13)
```

```
        unsafe {
            let odr =
core::ptr::read_volatile(GPIOC_ODR);
            core::ptr::write_volatile(GPIOC_ODR,
odr | (1 << 13));
        }

        delay(8_000_000);
    }
}

fn delay(cycles: u32) {
    for _ in 0..cycles {
        asm::nop();
    }
}
```

Let's walk through what each part does.

Step-by-Step Breakdown

Clock Enable (RCC AHB1ENR)
The STM32 uses a reset-and-clock-control unit to enable peripherals. GPIOC is attached to the AHB1 bus, and bit 2 of the RCC_AHB1ENR register enables the clock for GPIOC. If you skip this step, writing to the GPIO registers will have no effect.

GPIO Mode Configuration (MODER)
Every GPIO pin has a mode: input, output, alternate function, or analog. PC13 is controlled by bits 26 and 27 in the MODER register (because $13 \times 2 = 26$). Setting this to 01 makes it a general-purpose output.

Output Data (ODR)
The ODR register holds the actual output level. Setting bit 13 high drives PC13 high. Clearing it drives the pin low. The behavior of the LED depends on the board's electrical design, but on many STM32 boards, driving PC13 low turns the LED **on**, and high turns it **off**.

Delay Function
We use a busy-wait loop to create a delay between toggles. This is not precise and not power-efficient, but it demonstrates the concept clearly. For

more accurate timing, you'd use timers or the SysTick peripheral (which we'll cover separately).

Why Write Bare-Metal Firmware?

Using bare-metal access isn't always the best choice for maintainability or portability, but it's invaluable for:

- Understanding how microcontroller peripherals actually work
- Debugging startup code or bring-up routines
- Writing highly optimized or minimal firmware
- Working before HAL support exists for a given peripheral

It also helps you appreciate the structure and guarantees provided by PACs and HALs, which abstract over this kind of code while still letting you reach for it when needed.

Exercises

Try modifying the program in these ways to reinforce your understanding:

- Change the pin from PC13 to PA5 or another LED pin on your board.
- Change the delay to use a variable, and make the blink speed adjustable.
- Toggle multiple pins at once using a bitmask.
- Implement a delay that uses SysTick instead of busy-waiting.

Writing directly to memory-mapped registers may seem primitive at first, but in truth, it gives you full control over the hardware with minimal overhead. And in Rust, even this low-level code can be written with structure and confidence. You know exactly which bits you're touching, and why—and that's the kind of clarity that bare-metal programming is all about.

Timer-Based Delays and SysTick

When you're writing embedded firmware, timing control is often as critical as the logic itself. Whether you're implementing a debounce delay for a button, controlling the pulse width of an LED, or waiting for a sensor to stabilize, you need reliable delays that do not depend on vague `for` loops or arbitrary `nop` calls. This is where timers come in—and the simplest timer available on any ARM Cortex-M processor is **SysTick**.

The SysTick timer is part of the ARM Cortex-M core itself. It's always available, it's easy to configure, and it runs independently of your application code. When used properly, it provides millisecond-precise blocking delays or can be configured to trigger periodic interrupts for time-based tasks.

What Is SysTick?

SysTick is a 24-bit timer built into every ARM Cortex-M processor. It counts down from a reload value to zero and sets a flag (or triggers an interrupt) when it wraps. It runs from the processor clock, which means you can calculate time durations based on the known clock frequency.

Some key points:

- It decrements on each clock tick.
- You can use it in polling mode (check when it wraps).
- You can use it in interrupt mode (handle an ISR periodically).
- It's ideal for short to medium delays or system ticks.

You don't need to rely on any external peripheral to use it—it's available in every project targeting a Cortex-M chip.

Bare-Metal Example: Using SysTick for Delay

Let's say your system clock is running at 8 MHz. To generate a 1 millisecond delay, you want SysTick to count down from 8,000 to 0.

Here's a full example in `no_std` Rust using direct access to SysTick:

```
#![no_std]
#![no_main]

use cortex_m_rt::entry;
use cortex_m::peripheral::SYST;
use cortex_m::Peripherals;
use panic_halt as _;

#[entry]
fn main() -> ! {
    let mut peripherals =
Peripherals::take().unwrap();
    let syst = &mut peripherals.SYST;
```

69

```rust
    // System clock is 8 MHz, so 8,000 ticks = 1ms
    syst.set_reload(8_000 - 1);        // 1ms reload
    syst.clear_current();              // Clear
current value
    syst.enable_counter();             // Start the
timer

    loop {
        // Wait for COUNTFLAG to be set
        while !syst.has_wrapped() {}

        // Action every millisecond
        toggle_led(); // Example function (you'd
implement this)
    }
}
```

In this code:

- `set_reload()` configures the timer to count from 7999 to 0.
- `clear_current()` resets the counter register.
- `has_wrapped()` checks the COUNTFLAG, which is set when the timer hits zero.

You can scale this to wait longer durations simply by counting multiple ticks. For example, to wait 100ms, run this loop 100 times.

```rust
fn delay_ms(syst: &mut SYST, ms: u32) {
    for _ in 0..ms {
        while !syst.has_wrapped() {}
    }
}
```

Using SysTick With the HAL (Delay Abstraction)

In most embedded Rust projects, you won't need to use SysTick directly. The HAL provides a delay abstraction that wraps SysTick safely and efficiently.

Using the `stm32f4xx-hal`, here's a complete example:

```rust
#![no_std]
```

```rust
#![no_main]

use cortex_m_rt::entry;
use panic_halt as _;
use stm32f4xx_hal::{
    pac,
    prelude::*,
    delay::Delay,
};

#[entry]
fn main() -> ! {
    let dp = pac::Peripherals::take().unwrap();
    let cp =
cortex_m::Peripherals::take().unwrap();

    let rcc = dp.RCC.constrain();
    let clocks = rcc.cfgr.sysclk(8.mhz()).freeze();

    let mut delay = Delay::new(cp.SYST, clocks);

    let gpioc = dp.GPIOC.split();
    let mut led =
gpioc.pc13.into_push_pull_output();

    loop {
        led.set_low().unwrap();
        delay.delay_ms(500_u16);

        led.set_high().unwrap();
        delay.delay_ms(500_u16);
    }
}
```

In this version:

- The HAL sets up the system clock and wraps SysTick with a `Delay` struct.
- `delay_ms()` takes care of all the counter configuration for you.
- The result is a clean, readable loop that toggles the LED every 500 ms.

This abstraction is built on top of the same mechanisms we used earlier with direct SysTick access. It's just easier to work with, especially when you're using multiple timers or peripherals.

Delays vs. Real-Time Scheduling

SysTick delays are blocking—your processor isn't doing anything else while it waits. That's fine for simple firmware or during initialization, but it's not ideal for multitasking or power efficiency.

For more advanced applications, consider:

- Configuring SysTick to trigger **periodic interrupts**.
- Using **hardware timers** (like TIM2, TIM3) for scheduling and PWM.
- Using **RTIC** (Real-Time Interrupt-driven Concurrency) for task scheduling.

But at the early stages of firmware development—or in very constrained projects—blocking delays using SysTick are often the best trade-off for simplicity and timing accuracy.

Exercise: Building a Millisecond Timer

Try implementing a function that tracks time in milliseconds using SysTick interrupts. Here's the general outline:

1. Set up SysTick to fire every 1ms.
2. Implement a static counter in the interrupt handler.
3. Write a `millis()` function that returns the current value of that counter.

You'll need to:

- Enable the `SysTick` interrupt bit.
- Write a `#[exception] fn SysTick()` handler.
- Make the counter accessible through a `Mutex` or `atomic` primitive.

This turns SysTick into a real system tick—just like in Arduino's `millis()`.

SysTick is your most accessible timer on ARM Cortex-M devices. It's consistent, accurate, and supported by every chip and toolchain. Whether you use it directly or through a HAL, it gives you precise control over delays and scheduling from the very start of your firmware project. And once you're comfortable with it, you'll have the foundation you need to move on to advanced real-time behavior using interrupts, timers, and scheduling frameworks.

Chapter 5: Interrupts and Event-Driven Execution

As your firmware grows in complexity, you'll eventually hit a point where polling in loops isn't enough. You might be waiting for a sensor to trigger, a UART byte to arrive, or a timer to expire—and you don't want to waste precious CPU cycles checking flags in a loop. You want the processor to pause until something happens, then spring into action. This is where **interrupts** come in.

Interrupts let you respond to hardware or software events asynchronously. You configure a peripheral to generate an interrupt, write a function to handle it, and the processor will call that function automatically when the event occurs. It's a fundamental building block for real-time and low-power embedded applications.

What Are Interrupts and How They Work

In embedded systems, responsiveness and efficiency are everything. You don't have the luxury of wasting CPU cycles in long loops waiting for events. Whether it's a sensor triggering, a byte arriving over UART, or a timer rolling over, you want your system to react *as soon as* something happens. That's where interrupts come in.

An **interrupt** is a hardware signal that tells the processor to stop what it's doing and immediately handle a specific event. It's the embedded equivalent of tapping someone on the shoulder—you interrupt their current task to deal with something more urgent. The processor reacts by calling a predefined function known as an **Interrupt Service Routine (ISR)** or **interrupt handler**.

This mechanism allows your firmware to stay asleep, idle, or doing unrelated work, and only spring into action *when needed*. It's essential for event-driven execution, low-power operation, and building responsive systems.

How the Processor Handles an Interrupt

Here's what happens inside the processor the moment an interrupt is triggered:

1. The current instruction finishes executing.

2. The processor pushes some key registers onto the stack—like the program counter and status register—so it can later resume where it left off.
3. The processor disables further interrupts (unless nested interrupts are supported and enabled).
4. The processor looks up the address of the ISR from the **interrupt vector table**.
5. The ISR runs to completion.
6. The processor restores its saved state from the stack and resumes execution where it was interrupted.

All of this happens in just a few clock cycles on most Cortex-M chips.

Sources of Interrupts

Interrupts can be triggered by a wide variety of events. These include:

- **External interrupts** (e.g., a GPIO pin going high or low)
- **Peripheral interrupts** (e.g., UART receive complete, timer overflow, ADC conversion complete)
- **System interrupts** (e.g., SysTick, fault conditions)
- **Software interrupts** (e.g., exceptions like `PendSV`, or manually triggered events)

Each of these interrupt sources is associated with a unique identifier and, depending on the processor, may be assigned a priority.

Understanding the Interrupt Vector Table

The interrupt vector table is a lookup table stored at a fixed memory address—usually at the beginning of flash. Each entry corresponds to an interrupt source and contains the address of the function (ISR) that should be executed when that interrupt occurs.

The table looks something like this in memory:

```
0x0000_0000 → Stack Pointer (initial)
0x0000_0004 → Reset Handler
0x0000_0008 → NMI Handler
0x0000_000C → HardFault Handler
...
0x0000_0048 → TIM2 Handler
```

. . .

In Rust, you don't manage this table manually. The `cortex-m-rt` runtime and the device's PAC (Peripheral Access Crate) handle it for you. When you write:

```
#[interrupt]
fn TIM2() {
    // Your ISR code here
}
```

This function is automatically placed at the correct position in the vector table, corresponding to the TIM2 interrupt.

Example: A Timer Interrupt Flow

Let's take a common real-world example: you want to toggle an LED every second using a timer.

What needs to happen:

1. Configure the hardware timer (e.g., TIM2) to overflow every 1 second.
2. Enable its interrupt request line.
3. Define an ISR called `TIM2()` that will toggle the LED.
4. Tell the processor to unmask that interrupt in the NVIC (Nested Vectored Interrupt Controller).

Once that's done:

- The timer runs in the background.
- Every 1 second, it generates an interrupt.
- The processor stops what it's doing and calls `TIM2()`.
- Your ISR toggles the LED.
- The processor resumes its previous task.

The main loop can do anything else—or nothing at all. The toggling happens independently.

How Interrupts Differ from Polling

To illustrate the importance of interrupts, consider a button press.

Polling-based code:

```
loop {
    if gpio_pin.is_high() {
        handle_press();
    }
}
```

Interrupt-based code:

```
#[interrupt]
fn EXTI0() {
    handle_press();
}
```

The polling approach consumes CPU cycles continuously. The interrupt approach uses zero CPU until the button is actually pressed, and reacts immediately.

This difference translates to lower power consumption, faster reaction time, and cleaner design.

Things to Keep in Mind

- **Interrupts are non-blocking.** They should do their work quickly and exit. Avoid long delays or loops inside ISRs.
- **Interrupts should not allocate memory** or perform operations that might fail under resource constraints.
- **Do not share mutable data directly** between your main loop and ISR without synchronization.
- **You can mask or prioritize interrupts** using the NVIC to control how critical they are relative to one another.

We'll cover these aspects in later sections—but it's worth remembering early on that interrupts are powerful and essential, but they must be used responsibly.

Interrupts are the mechanism that lets your firmware respond to the outside world in real time. They let your code be reactive instead of wastefully proactive. In embedded Rust, defining, registering, and handling interrupts is clean, structured, and type-safe. And as you write more complex firmware, they'll become central to your architecture—whether you're handling sensors, communicating with peripherals, or running scheduled logic.

Writing and Registering Interrupt Handlers

Once you understand how interrupts work at a conceptual level, the next step is to define the exact behavior that should happen when an interrupt is triggered. This behavior is written in a function called an **interrupt handler**, or **Interrupt Service Routine (ISR)**. The job of this function is to respond to a specific event—such as a timer overflow or a button press—by executing logic quickly and safely.

In Rust, writing and registering an interrupt handler is straightforward, especially when using the `cortex-m-rt` crate in combination with your microcontroller's Peripheral Access Crate (PAC). Rust ensures that these handlers are properly placed into the interrupt vector table and gives you tools to write them without risking common embedded mistakes, such as unsafe access to shared memory or incorrect handler naming.

Declaring Interrupt Handlers with `#[interrupt]`

To define an interrupt handler in Rust, you use the `#[interrupt]` attribute provided by `cortex-m-rt`. This macro tells the runtime to associate your function with a specific interrupt vector, based on its name.

Here's a basic example for the Timer 2 interrupt (`TIM2`) on an STM32 microcontroller:

```
#[interrupt]
fn TIM2() {
    // This function will be called every time TIM2
triggers an interrupt
}
```

This function must have the exact name as the interrupt defined in the device's PAC. These names are typically listed in the documentation or the `pac::Interrupt` enum (e.g. `stm32f4::stm32f401::Interrupt`).

You don't need to register this function manually. When the binary is compiled, the `cortex-m-rt` linker script automatically places the address of this function in the correct position of the interrupt vector table.

Example: Timer-Based LED Toggle with TIM2

Let's put this into a practical use case. We want to configure Timer 2 to overflow every second and toggle an LED each time the interrupt fires.

```rust
#![no_std]
#![no_main]

use cortex_m_rt::entry;
use panic_halt as _;
use stm32f4xx_hal::{
    pac,
    prelude::*,
    timer::Timer,
    gpio::{gpioc::PC13, Output, PushPull},
};

use core::cell::RefCell;
use cortex_m::interrupt::Mutex;

static LED:
Mutex<RefCell<Option<PC13<Output<PushPull>>>>> =
Mutex::new(RefCell::new(None));

#[entry]
fn main() -> ! {
    let dp = pac::Peripherals::take().unwrap();
    let cp =
cortex_m::Peripherals::take().unwrap();

    let rcc = dp.RCC.constrain();
    let clocks = rcc.cfgr.sysclk(8.mhz()).freeze();

    let gpioc = dp.GPIOC.split();
    let led = gpioc.pc13.into_push_pull_output();

    cortex_m::interrupt::free(|cs| {
        LED.borrow(cs).replace(Some(led));
    });

    let mut timer = Timer::tim2(dp.TIM2, 1.hz(),
clocks);
```

```rust
    timer.listen();

    unsafe {

cortex_m::peripheral::NVIC::unmask(pac::Interrupt::
TIM2);
    }

    loop {
        // Main thread is idle
    }
}

#[interrupt]
fn TIM2() {
    use cortex_m::interrupt;

    interrupt::free(|cs| {
        if let Some(led) =
LED.borrow(cs).borrow_mut().as_mut() {
            led.toggle().ok();
        }
    });

    // Clear interrupt flag
    unsafe {
        (*pac::TIM2::ptr()).sr.modify(|_, w|
w.uif().clear());
    }
}
```

In this code:

- We use a global static `Mutex<RefCell<Option<PC13>>>` to share the LED between `main()` and the ISR safely.
- We initialize Timer 2 to trigger every 1 second.
- We enable its interrupt and unmask it in the NVIC.
- In the ISR, we toggle the LED and clear the interrupt flag so that the handler can be called again next time.

This is a complete example of how to write and register an interrupt handler in a production-grade Rust embedded firmware project.

Interrupt Safety Rules

Interrupts execute asynchronously, so you need to follow certain rules:

- Never block or perform long delays in an interrupt handler.
- Don't allocate heap memory or do anything that could panic inside an ISR.
- Keep handlers short and deterministic—do just enough work to capture the event, and let the main thread handle the rest.
- Clear the interrupt flag manually if your peripheral doesn't auto-clear it. If not cleared, the interrupt may fire continuously.

Verifying Your Handler Is Called

You can confirm that your handler is being executed in several ways:

- **Blink an LED** in the handler.
- **Toggle a GPIO pin** and check with a logic analyzer or oscilloscope.
- **Use a debug breakpoint** on the ISR function.
- **Output via serial (UART or RTT)** if available, though be careful about timing and buffer size.

You can also simulate faults to confirm that incorrect setups don't trigger interrupts as expected—this helps validate your initialization logic.

Summary of Setup Steps

For any interrupt you want to handle:

1. Enable the peripheral and configure it to generate interrupts (e.g., `timer.listen()`).
2. Define an interrupt handler function using `#[interrupt]`.
3. Use `cortex_m::peripheral::NVIC::unmask()` to enable the IRQ in NVIC.
4. (Optional) Set interrupt priority with `NVIC::set_priority()`.
5. In the handler, acknowledge or clear the interrupt flag.
6. Safely share data with `Mutex` or atomics if needed.

Writing interrupt handlers in embedded Rust is both low-level and well-structured. The language gives you tools to manage safety and shared access between contexts, and the ecosystem lets you define handlers with zero boilerplate. With a few lines of clear, well-written code, your system can start responding to real-time events as they occur—with precision and reliability.

NVIC Configuration and Prioritization

The Nested Vectored Interrupt Controller (NVIC) is an integral part of every ARM Cortex-M processor. It's the hardware block responsible for enabling, disabling, prioritizing, and dispatching interrupts to their respective handlers. Without configuring the NVIC properly, your interrupt-enabled peripherals won't behave as expected—even if you write the correct handlers and initialize the peripherals correctly.

In embedded Rust, interacting with the NVIC is clean and structured. This section will explain how the NVIC operates, how you configure it in Rust, and how to assign priorities to control which interrupts preempt others.

What the NVIC Controls

The NVIC provides fine-grained control over each interrupt line. Specifically, it allows you to:

- **Enable or disable individual interrupts**
- **Set interrupt priorities**
- **Clear pending interrupt flags**
- **Trigger interrupts via software**
- **Control whether an interrupt can preempt another**

Each peripheral interrupt (e.g., TIM2, USART1, EXTI0) has a corresponding entry in the NVIC. If that entry is disabled, the processor will never jump to the handler—even if the peripheral itself generates an interrupt request.

Enabling an Interrupt with NVIC

To enable an interrupt, you unmask it using:

```
use cortex_m::peripheral::NVIC;

unsafe {
    NVIC::unmask(pac::Interrupt::TIM2);
}
```

This tells the NVIC to allow the TIM2 interrupt to reach the processor when triggered. It does **not** automatically configure the peripheral—that must still be done with the PAC or HAL.

Unmasking an interrupt does not guarantee it will fire. You must:

1. Initialize the peripheral (e.g., configure Timer 2 to overflow).
2. Tell the peripheral to generate interrupts on the desired event.
3. Unmask the corresponding NVIC line as shown above.

If any of these steps is skipped, your handler won't be called.

Setting Interrupt Priority

Cortex-M processors support **interrupt priority levels**. Lower values represent **higher priority**. For example, an interrupt with priority 0 will preempt one with priority 2. The number of supported priority levels depends on the specific Cortex-M variant, but 4 to 8 levels is common.

You can set priority like this:

```
unsafe {
    let mut nvic =
cortex_m::peripheral::NVIC::steal();
    nvic.set_priority(pac::Interrupt::TIM2, 2);
}
```

This assigns a medium priority level to TIM2. If another interrupt is configured with priority 1, it can preempt TIM2 while it is executing.

Use `steal()` cautiously—it gives access to NVIC even if the compiler believes another reference exists. It's safe here because `NVIC` is a singleton in practice, but always avoid data races.

Real-World Example: Prioritizing Multiple Interrupts

Let's say you have a UART receiving data and a timer toggling an LED. You want the UART interrupt to take precedence, ensuring no characters are lost—even if the timer is active.

```
unsafe {
```

```
    let mut nvic =
cortex_m::peripheral::NVIC::steal();
    nvic.set_priority(pac::Interrupt::USART1, 1);
// higher priority
    nvic.set_priority(pac::Interrupt::TIM2, 3);
// lower priority

    NVIC::unmask(pac::Interrupt::USART1);
    NVIC::unmask(pac::Interrupt::TIM2);
}
```

Now, if both interrupts fire at the same time, the USART1 handler runs first. If the timer is executing and a UART byte arrives, the NVIC pauses the timer ISR, jumps to the UART handler, and resumes the timer ISR once the UART handler returns.

This preemptive behavior only applies if **nested interrupts are allowed**. The processor must have interrupts re-enabled within the ISR. In Rust, this can be done using:

```
cortex_m::interrupt::enable();
```

Place it cautiously—typically near the start of an ISR that can be preempted safely.

Software Triggering and Pending Management

You can **manually trigger** an interrupt by setting its pending bit:

```
NVIC::pend(pac::Interrupt::EXTI0);
```

This is useful for testing your handlers without requiring external hardware events. For example, triggering a software interrupt during startup to simulate a button press.

You can also clear a pending interrupt:

```
NVIC::unpend(pac::Interrupt::EXTI0);
```

Clearing pending flags may be needed after manual triggering or if you're resetting an interrupt configuration during runtime.

Disabling and Re-enabling Interrupts

To temporarily disable a specific interrupt:

```
cortex_m::peripheral::NVIC::mask(pac::Interrupt::TI
M2);
```

To re-enable it:

```
cortex_m::peripheral::NVIC::unmask(pac::Interrupt::
TIM2);
```

This is useful when updating configuration for a peripheral that may generate spurious interrupts during transition.

To globally disable all maskable interrupts:

```
cortex_m::interrupt::disable();
```

And to re-enable them:

```
cortex_m::interrupt::enable();
```

Use these global functions sparingly and for very short periods—like when accessing shared resources that are modified in both main and ISR contexts.

Exercise: Preempting a Low-Priority Timer With a High-Priority Button

1. Configure a timer to toggle an LED at 1Hz using a `TIM2` interrupt.
2. Configure an external interrupt (`EXTI0`) on a button press.
3. Set `EXTI0` to a higher priority than `TIM2`.
4. In the button ISR, briefly turn the LED off, then back on after 50ms.

This setup will demonstrate how a button press immediately interrupts the LED toggling, even if the timer ISR is executing. It's a clear way to observe interrupt preemption and NVIC prioritization in action.

The NVIC is your interface for managing interrupt behavior. It doesn't control what triggers an interrupt—that's the peripheral's job—but it controls *when* and *whether* the CPU responds. By setting priorities thoughtfully, you ensure that high-priority tasks—like receiving UART data—always get handled in time, and less critical tasks wait their turn. With Rust and the `cortex-m` crate, you get clear, structured access to all of this, with the compiler helping ensure you don't make low-level mistakes.

Sharing Data Between Main and ISRs Safely

One of the more subtle challenges in embedded development—especially when working with interrupts—is sharing data between your main application logic and interrupt service routines (ISRs). Since ISRs execute asynchronously, and may preempt your main code at any time, careless data sharing can lead to race conditions, inconsistent states, or memory corruption. These bugs are often intermittent and hard to trace.

Rust doesn't let you access global mutable state from multiple contexts without explicit synchronization. This is a good thing. It forces you to structure your code safely and predictably, even when handling asynchronous events.

The Problem: Concurrent Contexts

When an interrupt fires, it can preempt the main thread at any moment. If both the main thread and the ISR access the same memory—especially if one of them writes to it—you risk undefined behavior unless you protect the access.

Here's an example of what *not* to do:

```
static mut SHARED: u32 = 0;

fn main_loop() {
    unsafe {
        SHARED += 1;
    }
}

#[interrupt]
fn TIM2() {
    unsafe {
        SHARED += 1;
    }
}
```

This appears harmless, but it's not. Both accesses can happen simultaneously on a multi-cycle instruction like +=, leading to corrupted results. Worse, the compiler may reorder or optimize access in ways that break your assumptions.

Rust's unsafe is required here for a reason—this code is **not memory safe**.

To solve this, you need synchronization.

Option 1: Using cortex_m::interrupt::Mutex

The Mutex type from the cortex-m crate is designed specifically for sharing data between ISRs and the main thread. It disables interrupts temporarily while data is accessed, ensuring atomicity.

You typically pair Mutex with RefCell to allow interior mutability.

Here's a clean example:

```
use cortex_m::interrupt::{self, Mutex};
use core::cell::RefCell;

static SHARED_COUNTER: Mutex<RefCell<u32>> =
Mutex::new(RefCell::new(0));

fn increment_in_main() {
    interrupt::free(|cs| {
        *SHARED_COUNTER.borrow(cs).borrow_mut() +=
1;
    });
}

#[interrupt]
fn TIM2() {
    interrupt::free(|cs| {
        *SHARED_COUNTER.borrow(cs).borrow_mut() +=
1;
    });
}
```

The interrupt::free() block disables interrupts locally and provides a CriticalSection token (cs) that ensures no other code—interrupt or otherwise—can access that data at the same time. This guarantees exclusive, race-free access.

This approach is perfect when:

- You need to mutate shared state (e.g., buffers, counters, flags).
- The mutation is brief and infrequent.
- You don't need lock-free performance.

Option 2: Atomic Types for Lock-Free Access

If you're sharing a simple numeric value and don't need to store complex state, Rust's atomic types offer a lighter-weight and lock-free solution. They're ideal for counters, flags, and indexes.

```
use core::sync::atomic::{AtomicU32, Ordering};

static COUNT: AtomicU32 = AtomicU32::new(0);

fn main_task() {
    COUNT.fetch_add(1, Ordering::Relaxed);
}

#[interrupt]
fn TIM2() {
    COUNT.fetch_add(1, Ordering::Relaxed);
}
```

You can choose memory orderings:

- `Relaxed` (no ordering guarantees, fastest)
- `Acquire`, `Release`, `AcqRel` (enforce read/write visibility)
- `SeqCst` (strict total ordering)

In most embedded applications where ISR and main logic access the same data without relying on ordering relative to other operations, `Relaxed` is sufficient.

Use atomic types when:

- You're dealing with counters, flags, or single-word state.
- You want low-latency, lock-free access.
- You don't need to read-modify-write complex structures.

Option 3: Using `heapless` Queues or Buffers

In real-time systems, you often want to enqueue data in an ISR and process it in the main thread (or vice versa). The `heapless` crate provides `no_std` lock-free structures like `spsc::Queue`, `Vec`, and `RingBuffer`.

Example of a producer-consumer buffer:

```
# Cargo.toml
[dependencies]
heapless = "0.7"
use heapless::spsc::Queue;
use core::cell::RefCell;
use cortex_m::interrupt::{self, Mutex};

static QUEUE: Mutex<RefCell<Queue<u8, 8>>> =
Mutex::new(RefCell::new(Queue::new()));

fn enqueue_byte(b: u8) {
    interrupt::free(|cs| {
        let mut q = QUEUE.borrow(cs).borrow_mut();
        q.enqueue(b).ok(); // Ignore overflow
    });
}

#[interrupt]
fn USART1() {
    // Read byte from UART hardware here...
    let received = 42; // Placeholder
    enqueue_byte(received);
}
```

Then in `main()` you can:

```
loop {
    let byte = interrupt::free(|cs|
QUEUE.borrow(cs).borrow_mut().dequeue());
    if let Some(b) = byte {
        // Process the byte
    }
}
```

This setup gives you a fixed-capacity, lock-safe buffer between contexts—ideal for real-time communication without heap allocation.

Exercise: Shared Button Press Counter

1. Define a `static` atomic counter.
2. In the `EXTI0` ISR (external interrupt for a button), increment the counter.
3. In the main loop, read the counter and display its value on an LCD, serial console, or LED bar.

Use `AtomicU32` for the counter. Ensure the read in the main loop uses `load(Ordering::Relaxed)`.

This pattern demonstrates how to structure real-time event counting without locks or mutexes.

Summary of Patterns

- Use `Mutex<RefCell<>>` for structured access to complex shared state.
- Use `AtomicU*` for lightweight, single-value sharing.
- Use `heapless::Queue` or `RingBuffer` for ISR-safe producer-consumer designs.
- Avoid `static mut` unless it's truly isolated and access is externally synchronized.

Rust won't stop you from writing incorrect interrupt sharing code—but it **will** make you explicit about your risks. If you want mutable globals across contexts, you have to be intentional, and that's exactly what makes your code safer in the long run.

Sharing data between the main context and ISRs is where embedded systems start to get interesting—and where subtle bugs can hide if you're not careful. But with the right tools and approach, it's also where you build robust, responsive, and cleanly structured firmware.

Chapter 6: Serial Communication with UART

Serial communication is one of the oldest and most widely used forms of data transmission in embedded systems—and for good reason. It's simple, reliable, and well-supported across virtually every microcontroller platform. When you want to print debug messages, send commands, or communicate with another device like a GPS module or Bluetooth adapter, UART (Universal Asynchronous Receiver/Transmitter) is often your first tool.

In this chapter, you'll learn how to configure and use UART in Rust, how to send and receive data using both polling and interrupt-driven approaches, and how to leverage the serial interface for real-time debugging and logging. Everything you learn here will translate directly to real hardware and help you gain visibility into what your firmware is doing as it runs.

UART Configuration and Initialization

Before you can send or receive data over a serial line, your microcontroller's UART peripheral needs to be properly configured. This setup involves enabling the right hardware, selecting appropriate pins for transmission and reception, setting the correct baud rate, and initializing the peripheral in a mode that suits your communication needs. When done correctly, it becomes a rock-solid communication path between your device and any host system, peripheral module, or debugger tool.

Let's walk through the UART configuration process in Embedded Rust using the `stm32f4xx-hal`, targeting the popular STM32F401 microcontroller. This example applies broadly to any microcontroller in the STM32 family, and the same structure is mirrored in other HALs such as `nrf-hal`, `atsamd-hal`, or `rp2040-hal`.

Enabling the UART Peripheral

On the STM32F401, USART2 is commonly used for serial communication because it's mapped to PA2 (TX) and PA3 (RX) by default on many development boards like the Nucleo series.

Your first task is to configure the microcontroller's clocks and enable the GPIO ports used by the UART.

```
#![no_std]
#![no_main]

use cortex_m_rt::entry;
use panic_halt as _;
use stm32f4xx_hal::{
    pac,
    prelude::*,
    serial::{Serial, config::Config},
};
```

In your `main()` function, begin by setting up the clocks:

```
#[entry]
fn main() -> ! {
    let dp = pac::Peripherals::take().unwrap();
    let rcc = dp.RCC.constrain();
    let clocks =
rcc.cfgr.sysclk(84.mhz()).freeze();
```

You define a system clock frequency here (84 MHz in this case), which determines the timing for all peripherals—including UART. Precise clock configuration is essential because it directly impacts baud rate accuracy.

Setting Up GPIO Pins for UART

Next, configure the pins associated with the UART peripheral. On STM32F401:

- **PA2** is TX (Transmit)
- **PA3** is RX (Receive)

These pins must be set to *alternate function mode* because they're not GPIO by default when used for UART.

```
        let gpioa = dp.GPIOA.split();
        let tx_pin = gpioa.pa2.into_alternate();
        let rx_pin = gpioa.pa3.into_alternate();
```

The `into_alternate()` method configures the pins for the proper alternate function automatically inferred from their context. Internally, this sets the appropriate AFR (Alternate Function Register) bits in the GPIO peripheral.

Creating the UART Interface

Now you can construct the serial interface using the `Serial::usart2` function. This takes the USART2 peripheral, the two pins (TX and RX), a configuration object, and the clock object.

```
let serial = Serial::usart2(
    dp.USART2,
    (tx_pin, rx_pin),
    Config::default().baudrate(115_200.bps()),
    clocks,
).unwrap();
```

The `Config::default()` object provides sensible defaults:

- 8 data bits
- 1 stop bit
- No parity
- No hardware flow control

You can override these settings:

```
use stm32f4xx_hal::serial::config::{Config, Parity,
StopBits};

let config = Config::default()
    .baudrate(9600.bps())
    .parity(Parity::Even)
    .stopbits(StopBits::STOP2);
```

Once the serial peripheral is initialized, you split it into two halves—transmitter and receiver:

```
let (mut tx, mut rx) = serial.split();
```

This gives you a `tx` object that implements `embedded_hal::serial::Write<u8>` and an `rx` object that implements `embedded_hal::serial::Read<u8>`. These can be used for one-way or full-duplex communication.

Verifying the Setup: Echo Example

To test the UART configuration, a classic approach is to write an echo loop—read a byte, then immediately write it back.

```
loop {
    let received =
nb::block!(rx.read()).unwrap();
    nb::block!(tx.write(received)).ok();
    }
}
```

This will echo every byte you send from your PC terminal (like PuTTY, minicom, or TeraTerm) back to the screen. It verifies that:

- The UART peripheral is correctly initialized.
- The pins are correctly mapped.
- The clock configuration matches the expected baud rate.

You can now move on to printing messages, parsing commands, or building a UART-based protocol.

Common Initialization Mistakes and Fixes

- **Baud rate mismatch**: Always double-check that your terminal is configured to match the same baud rate (e.g., 115200) as your embedded code.
- **Wrong GPIO pins**: Refer to the datasheet or reference manual to verify which alternate function is needed for each pin.
- **Clock mismatch**: If your system clock is incorrectly configured, it will throw off all derived peripheral clocks, including UART.
- **Buffer overruns**: If you write too fast without reading incoming data, or vice versa, the hardware may signal an overrun error. Use interrupts or DMA if you need high throughput.

Exercise: Configurable Baud Rate UART Initialization

Try modifying your UART configuration to allow runtime selection of the baud rate using conditional compilation. Define a `const BAUD: u32` at the top and use `.baudrate(BAUD.bps())` in the config. Recompile with different values and observe how it changes communication behavior with your serial monitor.

Setting up UART properly is the key to unlocking interactive, transparent, and real-time communication between your embedded system and the outside world. Whether you're logging debug output, streaming data, or receiving structured commands, a clean and consistent initialization routine ensures your system communicates reliably—and that's the first step toward a professional, field-ready embedded firmware.

Transmitting and Receiving Data

Once your UART interface is initialized and connected, the next step is to actually use it for communication. Whether you're debugging firmware behavior, sending commands between devices, or streaming sensor data to a host PC, it all comes down to two core operations: **transmitting data** and **receiving data**.

In Embedded Rust, these operations are structured around traits provided by the `embedded-hal` crate—specifically `serial::Read` and `serial::Write`. These are implemented by UART drivers provided by your microcontroller's HAL, such as `stm32f4xx-hal`. These traits support non-blocking semantics by returning `nb::Result`, allowing your firmware to either poll, block, or integrate into interrupt-driven or async frameworks.

Transmitting Data

Transmitting data is straightforward: you send a byte using `.write(byte)`, and the UART peripheral places it in a transmission register. If the register is busy (i.e., still sending a previous byte), `.write()` returns a `WouldBlock` error, signaling you to try again later.

To write a single byte and wait until it's accepted:

```
nb::block!(tx.write(b'A')).unwrap();
```

The `nb::block!` macro keeps retrying until the transmission register is ready. It converts the non-blocking call into a blocking one, which is fine for occasional messages or initial bring-up tests.

Writing Strings

You can't write strings directly, since UART operates on bytes. To send a string, iterate through its bytes:

```
fn write_str<T:
embedded_hal::serial::Write<u8>>(tx: &mut T, s:
&str) {
    for byte in s.as_bytes() {
        nb::block!(tx.write(*byte)).ok();
    }
}
```

Usage:

```
write_str(&mut tx, "System ready.\r\n");
```

For repeated logging, wrap this in a `log_info()` function to prefix logs and ensure proper line endings.

Writing Data Efficiently

If you need to send many bytes, such as streaming a buffer or logging from a circular queue, avoid blocking for every byte. Instead, use either:

- An interrupt-based transmit buffer.
- DMA for high-throughput transmission.
- A polling loop that skips `WouldBlock` errors and writes as the UART becomes ready.

For polling:

```
for &byte in buffer.iter() {
    while let Err(nb::Error::WouldBlock) =
tx.write(byte) {}
}
```

Receiving Data

Receiving data works symmetrically. You call `.read()` on the `rx` object. If data is available, it returns a byte; if not, it returns `WouldBlock`.

```
if let Ok(byte) = rx.read() {
    // Handle the received byte
}
```

To block until a byte is received:

```
let received = nb::block!(rx.read()).unwrap();
```

This is acceptable in small systems but shouldn't be used if you need to maintain responsiveness or handle multiple inputs.

Buffered Reception

If you're polling `.read()` in your main loop, consider buffering incoming bytes to avoid loss. A simple approach is to use a ring buffer or a `heapless::spsc::Queue`.

```
use heapless::spsc::Queue;

let mut buffer: Queue<u8, 64> = Queue::new();

loop {
    if let Ok(byte) = rx.read() {
        buffer.enqueue(byte).ok(); // Ignore
overflow for now
    }

    if let Some(b) = buffer.dequeue() {
        process_byte(b);
    }
}
```

This gives you a basic form of UART reception decoupling—reading from hardware and processing data are independent, avoiding dropped bytes when your main loop is busy.

Echo Example: Full Transmit/Receive

Let's build a simple loopback system: read a byte, echo it back.

```
loop {
    let byte = nb::block!(rx.read()).unwrap();
    nb::block!(tx.write(byte)).ok();
}
```

This confirms end-to-end operation of both UART directions. With this setup, anything you type in your serial terminal should be echoed back immediately.

You can extend this to support line input, command parsing, or packetized communication.

Real-World UART Tips

- **Always match baud rates** between your microcontroller and host PC. 115200 is a good standard for development.
- **Handle line endings carefully**. Terminals often use \r\n; ensure your firmware does the same if you want clean output.
- **Avoid blocking on TX** if you're doing real-time work elsewhere. Use a buffer and flush it when idle.
- **Don't trust** `.read()` **to always be ready**—always check for `WouldBlock`.
- **Use logging over UART early in your development**. Even simple printouts help catch boot problems or logic errors.

Exercise: Input Command Handler

Write a handler that:

1. Collects incoming characters into a buffer.
2. When a newline is received (\n), processes the full line.
3. If the line is `"status"`, sends back `"OK\r\n"`.
4. If the line is `"reboot"`, prints `"Rebooting..."` and resets the microcontroller.

This introduces you to line-based parsing and string matching, two common tasks in UART command interfaces.

Transmitting and receiving bytes over UART may seem simple, but getting it right—especially under load or in a production setting—requires attention to timing, state management, and non-blocking patterns. Rust gives you the tools to structure your serial I/O in a way that's both robust and maintainable, whether you're sending debug logs or building an entire shell over UART.

Polling vs Interrupt-Driven Communication

When you're building a firmware system that uses UART—or any peripheral, really—how you handle data transfer can make or break performance. Two core models define how embedded systems typically interact with hardware peripherals: **polling** and **interrupt-driven communication**.

Both have their place. One is simple, direct, and predictable; the other is responsive, efficient, and concurrent. Understanding their differences helps you choose the right model for your application—and apply it correctly using Rust's embedded tools.

Polling: Constant Checking

Polling means your code manually checks whether an event has occurred. In UART terms, this means repeatedly calling .read() or .write() to see if data is ready to receive or if the hardware is ready to send.

This is usually done in the main loop:

```
loop {
    if let Ok(byte) = rx.read() {
        nb::block!(tx.write(byte)).ok(); // Echo
    }
}
```

This kind of loop can be useful in early development or simple applications where your firmware does little else. It's easy to reason about and doesn't require any interrupt configuration.

Pros of Polling

- Simple to implement
- Easier to debug (no asynchronous behavior)
- Useful for single-task firmware or initialization code

Cons of Polling

- CPU is constantly busy checking flags
- Wastes power
- Can't scale to multiple tasks effectively
- Risk of missing fast events if loop is delayed (e.g., with other work or blocking calls)

Polling is best when you have short, occasional messages and your main thread is mostly idle. But if you're doing anything time-sensitive, polling can become a bottleneck.

Interrupt-Driven Communication: Asynchronous and Efficient

With **interrupt-driven communication**, the peripheral itself triggers an event when it has data ready to read or space available to send. The CPU doesn't have to watch it constantly. Instead, it gets interrupted, temporarily jumps to a handler, and returns to what it was doing.

For UART, the typical interrupt events are:

- **RXNE** (Receive Not Empty): a byte has been received
- **TXE** (Transmit Data Register Empty): ready to send another byte

You enable interrupts like this:

```
serial.listen(stm32f4xx_hal::serial::Event::Rxne);
```

Then you define the handler:

```
use cortex_m::interrupt::Mutex;
use core::cell::RefCell;
use stm32f4xx_hal::pac::interrupt;

static UART_RX:
Mutex<RefCell<Option<stm32f4xx_hal::serial::Rx<pac:
:USART2>>>> =
    Mutex::new(RefCell::new(None));

#[interrupt]
fn USART2() {
    cortex_m::interrupt::free(|cs| {
        if let Some(rx) =
UART_RX.borrow(cs).borrow_mut().as_mut() {
```

```
            if let Ok(byte) = rx.read() {
                // Store or process byte
            }
        }
    });
}
```

Before you can use the interrupt, you must also:

1. Store the `Rx` object in a globally accessible `Mutex<RefCell<>>`
2. Unmask the NVIC interrupt line:

```
unsafe {

cortex_m::peripheral::NVIC::unmask(pac::Interrupt::
USART2);
}
```

This ensures the CPU is interrupted when a byte is received.

Pros of Interrupts

- Extremely efficient—CPU can sleep or do other work
- Great for low-power or multi-peripheral systems
- Ensures no data is missed (if buffer is large enough)
- Enables fast response to real-time events

Cons of Interrupts

- More complex setup
- Harder to debug than polling (due to asynchronous behavior)
- Risk of data races if shared state isn't synchronized correctly
- Handlers must be quick—no long computations or blocking

Interrupts are best when you care about responsiveness, power, or concurrency. They scale well and make your firmware more reactive—but they demand disciplined design.

When to Use Polling vs Interrupts

Use **polling** when:

- Your firmware is simple or doing only one task
- Data rates are low and occasional
- Power isn't a concern
- You want minimal setup

Use **interrupts** when:

- You want low latency and fast reaction
- You're juggling multiple I/O sources (e.g., UART + SPI + sensors)
- Data must not be lost (e.g., streaming UART at high baud rates)
- You care about CPU efficiency or power consumption

Often, real-world applications use a hybrid approach: interrupts receive data into a ring buffer, and the main loop reads from the buffer and processes it.

Example: Interrupt-Based UART Receive Buffer

Using `heapless::spsc::Queue`:

```
use heapless::spsc::Queue;

static BUFFER: Mutex<RefCell<Option<Queue<u8,
64>>>> =
    Mutex::new(RefCell::new(Some(Queue::new())));

#[interrupt]
fn USART2() {
    cortex_m::interrupt::free(|cs| {
        if let (Some(rx), Some(buf)) = (

UART_RX.borrow(cs).borrow_mut().as_mut(),
            BUFFER.borrow(cs).borrow_mut().as_mut()
        ) {
            if let Ok(byte) = rx.read() {
                buf.enqueue(byte).ok(); // ignore
overflow for now
            }
        }
    });
}
```

Then in your main loop:

```
loop {
    let byte_opt = cortex_m::interrupt::free(|cs| {

BUFFER.borrow(cs).borrow_mut().as_mut().unwrap().de
queue()
    });

    if let Some(b) = byte_opt {
        process_byte(b);
    }
}
```

This approach removes all busy-waiting. Your ISR fills a queue, and your application can process at its own pace.

Exercise: Compare Polling and Interrupt Performance

1. Set up a polling-based echo system at 115200 baud.
2. Switch to an interrupt-based version using a buffer.
3. Use a PC terminal or loopback test to send rapid characters.
4. Measure dropped characters, latency, and CPU usage (if supported).

You'll see that polling works—until it doesn't. Interrupts will handle spikes in input more reliably without stalling the rest of your program.

Polling and interrupt-driven I/O are both valid tools—what matters is how and when you use them. Start with polling to understand your hardware. Then move to interrupts as your needs grow. Embedded Rust gives you control over both models, along with the type safety and concurrency guarantees that make writing reliable firmware more than possible—it makes it pleasant.

Logging and Debugging Over Serial

When you're building firmware for an embedded system, especially in a no_std environment without access to a traditional console or file system, one of the most effective tools you have for visibility is the UART peripheral. Serial logging gives you a direct channel to observe your system in real time— from startup sequences to fault conditions and everything in between.

Logging over serial is about more than just printing strings; it's about instrumenting your firmware in a way that helps you understand what it's doing, verify that it's doing it correctly, and spot what goes wrong when it doesn't. In this section, we'll focus on structured, purposeful logging using UART, covering how to format, send, and manage log messages, along with how to use them effectively for live debugging.

Basic Serial Logging with UART

Assuming you've already configured your UART peripheral and obtained a `tx` handle, you can start with a very simple logging function:

```
fn log_str<T: embedded_hal::serial::Write<u8>>(tx:
&mut T, s: &str) {
    for byte in s.as_bytes() {
        nb::block!(tx.write(*byte)).ok();
    }
}
```

This function writes a string byte-by-byte using `embedded-hal`'s `Write<u8>` trait. While primitive, it's sufficient for simple boot-time messages and event tracing.

For instance:

```
log_str(&mut tx, "[BOOT] System initialized.\r\n");
```

This is immediately useful. If your system crashes or resets, you'll see where it reached in the output, giving you a timeline.

Building a Structured Logger

To make logging consistent and more expressive, wrap the `log_str` function with additional helpers:

```
fn log_info<T: embedded_hal::serial::Write<u8>>(tx:
&mut T, message: &str) {
    log_str(tx, "[INFO] ");
    log_str(tx, message);
    log_str(tx, "\r\n");
}
```

```
fn log_error<T:
embedded_hal::serial::Write<u8>>(tx: &mut T,
message: &str) {
    log_str(tx, "[ERROR] ");
    log_str(tx, message);
    log_str(tx, "\r\n");
}
```

This makes it easy to classify and filter log output in your terminal. You can later add timestamps, event IDs, or color coding if you're using a capable terminal emulator.

Using Logging in Practice

You should sprinkle logging strategically—at major execution milestones, before and after key hardware operations, and inside error handling paths. Some practical examples:

```
log_info(&mut tx, "Entering configuration mode.");
log_error(&mut tx, "Sensor not responding.");
```

You can even include numeric values by formatting strings before writing:

```
use core::fmt::Write;
use heapless::String;

let mut msg: String<64> = String::new();
write!(msg, "ADC reading: {}\r\n",
adc_value).unwrap();
log_str(&mut tx, &msg);
```

This requires the `heapless` crate, which gives you `no_std`-compatible, fixed-capacity strings.

Logging and Error Context

Logging isn't just for progress updates—it's essential for error tracing. When something fails, you should log:

- What was attempted
- The result or error code
- Any important configuration or state

For example:

```
if sensor.init().is_err() {
    log_error(&mut tx, "Sensor initialization
failed. Halting.");
    loop {} // stop safely
}
```

The serial log gives you post-mortem data if your firmware hangs or misbehaves.

Advanced Logging: `defmt` and RTT

For more sophisticated use cases, you can use **defmt**, a compact logging framework developed by the `probe-rs` and `embassy` teams. `defmt` minimizes log size by compressing messages and sending them via RTT (Real-Time Transfer).

Instead of writing strings byte-by-byte, you use macros:

```
defmt::info!("Starting system, clocks
configured.");
defmt::error!("Failed to read from EEPROM.");
```

`defmt` works with tools like `probe-run`, giving you structured logs in your terminal as the device runs. This is particularly useful when you want timestamped logs, log levels, and rich formatting without large binary size overhead.

Debugging Over Serial

Besides logging, you can use the UART port to:

- Print register values and sensor data
- Display error codes
- Stream performance counters (like loop timing or memory use)
- Echo commands or responses for testing communication
- Simulate shell-like input from the terminal

For instance, during initialization:

```
log_info(&mut tx, "Configuring I2C at 400kHz...");
```

After initialization:

```
if i2c_status != Ok(()) {
    log_error(&mut tx, "I2C failed during bus
scan.");
}
```

If your system locks up unexpectedly, having a record of the last successful log messages can point you to the precise moment of failure.

Exercise: Serial-Based Panic Reporting

1. Implement a `panic_handler` that writes a message to UART before halting:

```
use core::panic::PanicInfo;

#[panic_handler]
fn panic(info: &PanicInfo) -> ! {
    use core::fmt::Write;
    use heapless::String;

    let mut msg: String<128> = String::new();
    write!(msg, "PANIC: {}\r\n", info).ok();
    log_str(&mut UART, &msg); // UART is your
configured tx

    loop {}
}
```

2. Trigger a panic intentionally with `panic!("Test failure")` and confirm the output in your serial terminal.

This is a practical way to make panic information available even in production builds, where JTAG/SWD debugging may not be an option.

Serial logging is your embedded system's voice. It tells you what's happening inside a black box—without interfering with its real-time behavior. Used thoughtfully, it becomes an essential tool for diagnostics, testing, and validation. Whether you're writing your own basic formatter or using a professional-grade framework like `defmt`, what matters is that you use it consistently to make your firmware more observable, more predictable, and ultimately more reliable.

Chapter 7: I2C, SPI, and Analog Interfaces

As your firmware grows beyond blinking LEDs and handling serial input, the next logical step is to start interacting with external devices—sensors, displays, memory chips, wireless modules, and more. These peripherals connect over a variety of buses, the most common of which are **I2C**, **SPI**, and **analog** interfaces. Each of these serves a different purpose and has a different communication model, but with the right setup, Embedded Rust makes working with them structured, safe, and efficient.

This chapter focuses on how to use Rust to set up and work with I2C and SPI peripherals, read analog data using an ADC, and convert the raw input into usable values. You'll see practical examples of wiring up external sensors, managing bus protocols, and dealing with errors in a way that keeps your firmware reliable and maintainable.

Communicating with External Devices

At the core of many embedded applications is the ability to talk to something outside the microcontroller—whether it's a temperature sensor, flash memory chip, display, or a wireless module. These devices are often simple and focused in function, but their interaction protocols must be handled precisely. Communication errors at this level usually translate to bad readings, unresponsive peripherals, or outright system failure.

The main digital interfaces for connecting to external devices in embedded systems are I2C, SPI, and UART. For analog sensors, we rely on ADCs (Analog-to-Digital Converters) to read voltage levels and interpret them as real-world values. Each of these interfaces requires specific configuration, timing considerations, and structured communication to work reliably.

To communicate with an external peripheral, you're physically wiring your microcontroller's I/O pins to the pins of another device. That connection needs to meet certain conditions:

- The voltage levels must match (3.3V or 5V logic)
- Pull-up or pull-down resistors may be needed (especially for I2C)

- Communication lines must be mapped to the correct peripheral (e.g., I2C1 vs I2C2)

For digital interfaces like I2C and SPI, communication is typically **master-slave** (or master-client). The microcontroller initiates all transfers and controls the clock. The external device responds according to the protocol.

For analog sensors, the microcontroller passively samples a voltage level on an analog-capable pin.

Structuring Communication in Rust

Rust encourages clear separation of concerns. When working with external devices, you should strive to encapsulate communication logic in reusable, testable driver modules.

Let's say you're working with an I2C-connected temperature sensor. Start by identifying what the sensor expects:

- An I2C address (e.g., 0x48)
- A register to read temperature (e.g., 0x00)
- Data format (e.g., 2 bytes, big-endian, 0.0625°C per bit)

Now structure a driver:

```
pub struct TempSensor<I2C> {
    i2c: I2C,
    address: u8,
}

impl<I2C, E> TempSensor<I2C>
where
    I2C:
embedded_hal::blocking::i2c::WriteRead<Error = E> +
embedded_hal::blocking::i2c::Write<Error = E>,
{
    pub fn new(i2c: I2C, address: u8) -> Self {
        Self { i2c, address }
    }

    pub fn read_temperature(&mut self) ->
Result<f32, E> {
```

```
        let mut buffer = [0u8; 2];
        self.i2c.write_read(self.address, &[0x00],
&mut buffer)?;

        let raw = ((buffer[0] as u16) << 8 |
buffer[1] as u16) >> 4;
        let temp = raw as f32 * 0.0625;
        Ok(temp)
    }
}
```

This abstraction allows you to:

- Isolate protocol logic from the rest of your firmware
- Reuse the driver across platforms
- Mock or test sensor behavior in software

Polling a Device: A Full Example

Let's tie this together with a concrete usage example in `main()`:

```
let dp = pac::Peripherals::take().unwrap();
let rcc = dp.RCC.constrain();
let clocks = rcc.cfgr.freeze();

let gpiob = dp.GPIOB.split();
let scl =
gpiob.pb8.into_alternate().set_open_drain();
let sda =
gpiob.pb9.into_alternate().set_open_drain();

let i2c = I2c::new(dp.I2C1, (scl, sda), 100.khz(),
clocks);

let mut sensor = TempSensor::new(i2c, 0x48);

loop {
    match sensor.read_temperature() {
        Ok(t) => {
            log_info(&mut tx,
&format_args!("Temperature: {:.2} °C", t));
        }
```

```
        Err(_) => {
            log_error(&mut tx, "Failed to read
temperature.");
        }
    }

    delay.delay_ms(1000u32);
}
```

This gives you a clean main loop where the logic focuses on **what** to do, not **how** the bits move. The actual I2C logic lives inside the sensor driver, keeping your main loop readable and maintainable.

Timing and Protocol Considerations

Every device has timing requirements. Some devices need a delay between commands, or they'll ignore or corrupt data. Some I2C sensors need a minimum clock stretching time. SPI peripherals may have strict setup and hold times around the chip select line.

To prevent issues:

- Read the datasheet thoroughly
- Always check timing diagrams
- Insert small delays if needed using HAL delay abstractions
- Make sure the peripheral clock is fast enough to meet timing specs

Exercise: Write Your Own Device Driver

Pick a simple I2C or SPI device—such as:

- A BME280 (temperature, pressure, humidity)
- An AT24C EEPROM chip
- A MAX7219 7-segment LED controller

Implement a `new()`, `read()`, and `write()` method. Use `embedded-hal` traits to keep it generic. Test the driver with a basic loop that polls every second and logs output over UART.

Debugging Peripheral Communication

When something goes wrong—no response, garbage data, or timeouts—check these in order:

1. **Physical connections**: Wrong pins or loose wires?
2. **Power and logic level**: 5V sensor on a 3.3V board?
3. **Peripheral config**: Right alternate function and mode?
4. **Clock speed**: Too fast for the device?
5. **Addressing**: Is the I2C address correct and shifted properly?
6. **Bus analyzer**: Use a logic analyzer or oscilloscope to watch the bus if needed.

Rust's type system won't save you from a bad wire, but its explicit error handling helps you isolate what went wrong—and where.

Talking to external devices is what makes your microcontroller system useful. Rust's approach to embedded development—generic traits, structured drivers, and explicit results—gives you everything you need to build reliable and scalable device integrations. Whether it's reading a voltage from a temperature sensor, configuring a display, or streaming data from a motion sensor, communication becomes more about logic and less about guesswork when you follow these practices.

Implementing I2C and SPI Drivers

In embedded development, I2C and SPI are the foundational protocols for communicating with most external chips—sensors, displays, memory, or DACs. While your HAL may offer ready-to-use peripheral abstractions, building your own drivers—especially device-specific drivers—is what gives you control, modularity, and long-term maintainability.

A well-structured driver in Rust should abstract the low-level protocol details and expose a clean, intuitive interface. It should be reusable across boards, unit-testable in logic, and precise in handling communication edge cases. With Rust's trait system and strong typing, you're able to design drivers that are generic over transport (I2C or SPI) but still concrete in functionality.

Foundation: Using `embedded-hal` Traits

To ensure your drivers are portable across architectures and platforms, they should depend on traits defined in the `embedded-hal` crate.

For I2C:

```
use embedded_hal::blocking::i2c::{Write,
WriteRead};
```

For SPI:

```
use embedded_hal::blocking::spi::Transfer;
use embedded_hal::digital::v2::OutputPin;
```

These are the core building blocks for communication: sending commands, reading responses, and asserting chip select.

I2C Driver: Temperature Sensor (e.g., TMP102)

The TMP102 is a digital temperature sensor with a simple I2C interface. It uses a 7-bit address (typically `0x48`), and its temperature register is at offset `0x00`.

Here's how you would write a minimal driver for it:

```
pub struct Tmp102<I2C> {
    i2c: I2C,
    address: u8,
}

impl<I2C, E> Tmp102<I2C>
where
    I2C: WriteRead<Error = E> + Write<Error = E>,
{
    pub fn new(i2c: I2C, address: u8) -> Self {
        Self { i2c, address }
    }

    pub fn read_temperature(&mut self) ->
Result<f32, E> {
        let mut buffer = [0u8; 2];
        self.i2c.write_read(self.address, &[0x00],
&mut buffer)?;

        let raw = ((buffer[0] as u16) << 4) |
((buffer[1] as u16) >> 4);
```

```
        let temp_celsius = raw as f32 * 0.0625;

        Ok(temp_celsius)
    }

    pub fn destroy(self) -> I2C {
        self.i2c
    }
}
```

This driver:

- Sends a single-byte command (0x00) to select the temperature register
- Reads two bytes and converts them to a Celsius value
- Owns the I2C bus and provides a destroy() method to release it

In your main application:

```
let i2c = I2c::new(dp.I2C1, (scl, sda), 100.khz(),
clocks);
let mut sensor = Tmp102::new(i2c, 0x48);

let temp = sensor.read_temperature().unwrap();
log_info(&mut tx, &format_args!("Temperature: {:.2}
°C", temp));
```

This abstraction keeps your main code clean and your sensor communication encapsulated.

SPI Driver: Flash Memory (e.g., W25Q32)

Let's say you're working with a Winbond SPI Flash. It speaks via commands like:

- 0x9F: Read JEDEC ID (returns 3 bytes)
- 0x03: Read data
- 0x06: Write enable
- 0x02: Page program

You'll need to manage SPI transactions and the CS line manually.

```
pub struct Flash<SPI, CS> {
```

```
    spi: SPI,
    cs: CS,
}

impl<SPI, CS, E> Flash<SPI, CS>
where
    SPI: Transfer<u8, Error = E>,
    CS: OutputPin,
{
    pub fn new(spi: SPI, cs: CS) -> Self {
        Self { spi, cs }
    }

    pub fn read_jedec_id(&mut self) -> Result<[u8;
3], E> {
        let mut cmd = [0x9F, 0, 0, 0];

        self.cs.set_low().ok();
        self.spi.transfer(&mut cmd)?;
        self.cs.set_high().ok();

        Ok([cmd[1], cmd[2], cmd[3]])
    }

    pub fn destroy(self) -> (SPI, CS) {
        (self.spi, self.cs)
    }
}
```

Usage:

```
let flash = Flash::new(spi, cs);
let id = flash.read_jedec_id().unwrap();
log_info(&mut tx, &format_args!("JEDEC ID: {:02X}
{:02X} {:02X}", id[0], id[1], id[2]));
```

Here, the `Flash` struct handles the protocol quirks of the device and exposes only safe, readable methods to the application.

Driver Design Guidelines

When implementing drivers:

- Own the bus (I2C/SPI) and pins if possible. Let the driver manage them.
- Provide a `destroy()` method to release ownership.
- Use `Result` types to propagate transport errors up the stack.
- Avoid exposing low-level registers unless absolutely necessary.
- Prefer named methods (`read_temperature`, `read_id`) over raw byte arrays.

Testing Drivers in Isolation

Although you're likely developing on embedded hardware, it helps to test your logic on a PC or in CI environments.

Use the `embedded-hal-mock` crate:

```
[dev-dependencies]
embedded-hal-mock = "0.8"
```

Then simulate I2C reads:

```
use embedded_hal_mock::i2c::{Mock as I2cMock,
Transaction as I2cTransaction};

let expectations = [
    I2cTransaction::write_read(0x48, vec![0x00],
vec![0x1A, 0x40])
];
let mock = I2cMock::new(&expectations);

let mut sensor = Tmp102::new(mock, 0x48);
assert_eq!(sensor.read_temperature().unwrap(),
26.25);
```

This lets you verify that your driver behaves correctly, even before wiring up real hardware.

Exercise: Build and Integrate an I2C EEPROM Driver

1. Implement a struct for AT24C02 EEPROM with `read_byte(addr)` and `write_byte(addr, value)` methods.
2. Use `write_read()` for reads and `write()` for writes.

3. Test the driver with a simple loop that writes then reads a value, verifying correctness with UART output.

You'll gain practice with timing (e.g., EEPROM write delay), addressing schemes, and stateful protocols.

Writing drivers in Embedded Rust is about clarity and safety. By wrapping low-level I2C and SPI protocols inside well-structured abstractions, you create reusable, testable, and reliable modules. Whether you're reading sensor values, configuring a display, or storing data in flash, building drivers this way ensures each device behaves exactly as expected—and that your firmware stays clean and maintainable as your system grows.

Reading Sensor Data via ADC

Not all sensors speak digital. Many expose their readings as analog voltages— an output that varies linearly (or sometimes logarithmically) with temperature, pressure, light, or some other physical quantity. To interpret these voltages in firmware, you use an **Analog-to-Digital Converter (ADC)**.

The ADC is a peripheral that samples a voltage level on a designated pin and converts it into a digital number. This number represents the voltage relative to a known reference—typically the supply voltage (e.g., 3.3V or 5V). In Rust, especially when using a HAL like `stm32f4xx-hal`, reading from the ADC is safe, cleanly abstracted, and surprisingly straightforward. But to make practical use of that reading, you also need to understand how to configure the ADC, scale the result, and map it to meaningful physical values.

ADC Basics and Configuration

Let's use the STM32F4 family for a concrete example. It features a 12-bit ADC that outputs values in the range `0-4095`, where `0` corresponds to 0V and `4095` corresponds to the ADC's reference voltage (typically 3.3V or Vref).

You begin by configuring the pin you want to sample as an analog input. For example, PA0 on many STM32 boards is connected to ADC channel 0:

```
let gpioa = dp.GPIOA.split();
let mut adc_pin = gpioa.pa0.into_analog();
```

Then configure the ADC itself:

```
use stm32f4xx_hal::adc::{Adc, config::AdcConfig};
```

```
let mut adc = Adc::adc1(dp.ADC1, true, AdcConfig::default());
```

You now have everything you need to take a reading:

```
let value: u16 = adc.read(&mut adc_pin).unwrap();
```

The value returned is a raw ADC count between 0 and 4095.

Converting ADC Values to Voltage

To make sense of this number, convert it into a voltage. Assuming a 3.3V reference:

```
fn adc_to_voltage(adc_value: u16) -> f32 {
    let max_adc = 4095.0;
    let v_ref = 3.3;
    (adc_value as f32 / max_adc) * v_ref
}
```

You can now log it:

```
let v = adc_to_voltage(value);
log_info(&mut tx, &format_args!("Sensor voltage:
{:.3} V", v));
```

This is especially useful when debugging or calibrating your analog circuit.

Reading a Temperature Sensor

Let's say you've connected an analog temperature sensor like the TMP36 to PA0. According to the datasheet:

- 0.5V = 0°C
- Each 10mV above 0.5V = +1°C

So, 750mV = 25°C, and so on.

To convert the voltage:

```
fn voltage_to_celsius(v: f32) -> f32 {
    (v - 0.5) * 100.0
}
```

Combined usage:

```
let raw = adc.read(&mut adc_pin).unwrap();
let voltage = adc_to_voltage(raw);
let temp = voltage_to_celsius(voltage);

log_info(&mut tx, &format_args!("Temperature: {:.1}
°C", temp));
```

This structure keeps your code clean and separates hardware reading from application logic.

Sample Timing and Oversampling

The ADC peripheral takes time to complete a conversion. On STM32, this depends on your ADC clock and sampling time configuration. If you sample too quickly, you risk noisy or inaccurate readings—especially for high-impedance sources.

To reduce noise and improve stability:

- Increase sampling time (most HALs default to a safe mid-range value)
- Take multiple readings and average them
- Avoid reading immediately after switching channels (settling time)

Example averaging:

```
fn read_avg(adc: &mut Adc<ADC1>, pin: &mut impl
embedded_hal::adc::Channel<ADC1, ID=u8>) -> u16 {
    let mut sum = 0u32;
    for _ in 0..8 {
        sum += adc.read(pin).unwrap() as u32;
    }
    (sum / 8) as u16
}
```

Use this in place of a single read when precision is more important than speed.

Exercise: Voltage Divider Measurement

Set up a voltage divider with a known resistor (e.g., 10kΩ) and a variable resistor (e.g., light-dependent resistor or thermistor) between 3.3V and GND. Connect the center point to PA0.

1. Read the ADC value.
2. Convert it to voltage.
3. Calculate the resistance of the unknown resistor.
4. Print the result over UART.

This teaches you how to use ADCs for indirect measurement of resistance, a common pattern in sensor interfacing.

Common Mistakes and Fixes

- **Wrong pin mode**: Make sure the pin is set to analog. Leaving it as a digital input or alternate function can lead to garbage readings.
- **Noisy power supply**: Use decoupling capacitors. ADCs are sensitive to ripple.
- **Floating inputs**: Always connect analog inputs to a valid voltage source—even if it's a pulldown resistor.
- **Improper reference**: Don't assume the reference voltage is always 3.3V. Some boards have different supply levels, or the reference may vary under load.

If readings are erratic, first confirm with a multimeter. If they still mismatch, slow down the sampling time and double-check your Vref assumptions.

Reading data via ADC is your bridge between the digital and analog world. Rust's embedded ecosystem gives you a clean, high-level interface for low-level operations, while ensuring safety and predictability. Once you understand how to convert raw values into real numbers—and how to structure that logic in reusable functions—you can unlock a wide range of sensor applications with confidence.

From battery monitoring and temperature sensing to analog control and diagnostics, mastering ADC usage in Rust gives your firmware eyes to observe the physical world and respond to it with clarity.

Error Handling and Data Conversion

When your firmware interacts with external devices—whether it's an I2C sensor, SPI flash chip, or an analog signal read through an ADC—failures can and will happen. Wires disconnect. Devices power up late. Data doesn't always come back the way you expect. Your job isn't just to get the happy path working, but to build systems that can recognize when something goes wrong, respond meaningfully, and recover cleanly.

In Rust, error handling is explicit. Instead of returning ambiguous codes or silently failing, functions return `Result` types that must be handled. This makes your code safer, more predictable, and more honest. Combined with strong typing and the absence of nulls or exceptions, Rust gives you clear control over both data integrity and operational correctness.

Handling Peripheral Communication Errors

Let's say you're using I2C to talk to a temperature sensor:

```
let mut buffer = [0u8; 2];
match i2c.write_read(0x48, &[0x00], &mut buffer) {
    Ok(_) => {
        // Successful read
    }
    Err(e) => {
        log_error(&mut tx, "I2C read failed.");
        // Optional: retry or enter safe fallback
    }
}
```

The `write_read()` method returns a `Result<(), E>` where `E` is typically an enum of error types (like NACK, bus error, or timeout).

You can act based on the specific error:

```
match i2c.write_read(0x48, &[0x00], &mut buffer) {
    Ok(_) => { /* all good */ }
    Err(e) => match e {
        embedded_hal::i2c::Error::Nack =>
log_error(&mut tx, "Device not responding."),
```

```
            embedded_hal::i2c::Error::Bus =>
log_error(&mut tx, "I2C bus error."),
        _ => log_error(&mut tx, "Other I2C
error."),
    }
}
```

Even if the HAL wraps error types into a custom error enum, you can destructure and match accordingly. Always log the error, and consider implementing a retry mechanism for transient failures.

Safe Fallback and Recovery Patterns

Let's say you're trying to read temperature, and the I2C bus fails. Instead of crashing or freezing, you can return a default or an error code to the rest of your application:

```
fn get_temperature(i2c: &mut I2C) -> Result<f32,
&'static str> {
    let mut buffer = [0u8; 2];
    i2c.write_read(0x48, &[0x00], &mut buffer)
        .map_err(|_| "Sensor read failed")?;

    let raw = ((buffer[0] as u16) << 4) |
((buffer[1] as u16) >> 4);
    Ok(raw as f32 * 0.0625)
}
```

Now, your caller knows whether the temperature was valid:

```
match get_temperature(&mut i2c) {
    Ok(temp) => log_info(&mut tx,
&format_args!("Temperature: {:.2} °C", temp)),
    Err(msg) => log_error(&mut tx, msg),
}
```

This is the idiomatic way to propagate and handle errors in Embedded Rust. It keeps logic clear and prevents false assumptions about hardware state.

ADC Value Scaling and Clipping

Raw ADC values are meaningless on their own. A reading of 2048 tells you nothing unless you know:

- The ADC's reference voltage
- The bit resolution (e.g., 12-bit, 10-bit)
- The electrical characteristics of the sensor

Let's say you're reading from a TMP36 analog temperature sensor on a 3.3V reference, and the ADC returns 2250:

```
fn adc_to_voltage(adc_value: u16, vref: f32) -> f32
{
    (adc_value as f32 / 4095.0) * vref
}

fn voltage_to_celsius(voltage: f32) -> f32 {
    (voltage - 0.5) * 100.0
}
```

Combined usage:

```
let raw = adc.read(&mut channel).unwrap();
let voltage = adc_to_voltage(raw, 3.3);
let temp = voltage_to_celsius(voltage);
```

This approach keeps conversions testable and unit-consistent. You can now mock or unit test the math independently of the hardware.

Handling Out-of-Range Values

Sensors can produce values outside expected ranges due to:

- Faulty wiring
- Incorrect scaling
- Sensor failure
- Floating analog inputs

Always validate your data before using it:

```
if !(15.0..=45.0).contains(&temp) {
    log_error(&mut tx, "Temperature out of expected range.");
```

```
}
```

For mission-critical applications, set upper and lower bounds for every input. This prevents propagation of bad data downstream.

Converting Binary Sensor Data

Many digital sensors return packed binary values—multi-byte sequences representing fixed-point or signed data. Here's how to safely unpack:

Example: 16-bit signed value, big-endian

```
fn parse_signed_16bit_be(high: u8, low: u8) -> i16
{
    i16::from_be_bytes([high, low])
}
```

Use it after reading from a sensor like MPU6050:

```
let mut buf = [0u8; 2];
i2c.write_read(ADDR, &[0x3B], &mut buf).unwrap();
let accel_x = parse_signed_16bit_be(buf[0],
buf[1]);
```

Now scale it based on your sensitivity:

```
let accel_x_g = accel_x as f32 / 16384.0;
```

This keeps the raw and scaled data decoupled, making your driver cleaner and more reusable.

Exercise: Normalize and Validate Sensor Input

1. Connect a linear analog sensor (potentiometer or light sensor).
2. Read the ADC value.
3. Convert to voltage and normalize to a 0.0–1.0 float.
4. Log a warning if the value is below 0.1 or above 0.9.
5. Send scaled data via UART as a percentage.

This exercise ties together raw data acquisition, conversion, scaling, and logical validation—all critical in real-world sensor applications.

Error handling and data conversion are two sides of the same responsibility: **ensuring that the information your firmware acts on is valid, meaningful, and correct**. Embedded Rust equips you with tools that make these responsibilities explicit, enforceable, and safe—eliminating many of the bugs that plague embedded systems written in less disciplined languages.

Whether you're dealing with a glitch on the bus, a misread voltage, or unexpected binary formats, handling failure and interpreting raw data with care is what sets robust firmware apart from fragile demos. And with well-structured, clear code, your system not only functions—it can be trusted.

Chapter 8: Power Efficiency and Sleep Modes

Power consumption is a critical consideration in embedded systems—especially when you're designing for battery-powered devices, long-term deployments, or energy-sensitive applications like wearable health trackers, environmental monitors, and IoT sensors. Unlike traditional desktop applications, embedded firmware doesn't get to assume a wall socket is always nearby.

Modern microcontrollers are highly capable of adapting their power usage to match workload demand. They support multiple low-power states, can shut down unused peripherals, and allow fine-grained control over wake-up behavior. Rust's embedded ecosystem provides safe, structured access to these features, enabling you to design firmware that's both responsive and efficient.

Overview of Microcontroller Power States

When you're working on an embedded device—especially one powered by a battery or designed for long-term deployment—minimizing power consumption isn't just a nice-to-have. It's essential. You don't want your sensor node dying after a few days. You want it to last months or years, and to do that, your microcontroller has to be smart about how and when it consumes energy.

Microcontrollers provide a range of built-in **power states** that let you control what parts of the system stay active and what shuts down. By shifting between these states based on activity, your firmware can stay efficient without sacrificing responsiveness. But it requires a clear understanding of what each state does, how transitions work, and what you lose or retain at each level.

Run Mode

This is the normal operating state of the microcontroller.

- The CPU is actively executing code.
- All peripherals are powered and operational.
- The system clock runs at full speed.

It's the most power-hungry state, consuming tens of milliamps depending on your clock speed and voltage. In Rust-based firmware, any time you're inside your `loop {}` running logic, you're in run mode.

Run mode is necessary when you're:

- Handling complex computations
- Transmitting over UART, SPI, or I2C
- Doing time-sensitive operations (e.g., PWM updates)
- Waiting for short-duration hardware responses

But once you're done, you should exit it as soon as possible to save energy.

Sleep Mode

Sleep mode is the first level of power reduction. In this mode:

- The **CPU clock is stopped,** halting instruction execution.
- **Peripherals continue to run**—timers, UART, ADC, etc.
- The CPU resumes on any **enabled interrupt**.

You enter sleep mode using:

```
use cortex_m::asm;
asm::wfi(); // Wait For Interrupt
```

This is a very efficient trade-off: you stop running code, but peripherals stay active. It's perfect for short idling:

- Waiting for UART data
- Delaying between samples
- Monitoring a GPIO pin for input

Example:

```
loop {
    check_status();
    asm::wfi(); // Enter sleep while waiting for
external event
}
```

Power consumption drops significantly—often into the low hundreds of microamps.

Stop Mode (or Deep Sleep)

Stop mode is a deeper sleep state. In this mode:

- **All system clocks are stopped**, including the main oscillator.
- **RAM contents are preserved.**
- **Most peripherals are disabled**, but low-power ones may remain (e.g., RTC).
- The CPU wakes from external interrupts or timer alarms.

You enable it by setting the SLEEPDEEP bit:

```
use cortex_m::peripheral::SCB;

SCB::set_sleepdeep();
asm::wfi(); // Enter Stop mode
```

This mode is ideal when:

- You want to wake every few seconds or minutes
- Your system waits for a sensor interrupt or external pin change
- You don't need to do background tasks while idle

On STM32 chips, power drops into the single-digit microamp range—perfect for battery conservation.

However, be aware that:

- You need to reconfigure clocks after wakeup
- Wakeup is slower than from sleep mode
- Only certain interrupts (e.g., EXTI, RTC, LPTIM) can wake the CPU

Standby Mode

Standby is the deepest sleep state available on most MCUs.

- **All clocks and RAM are shut down.**
- **Only wakeup pins or RTC alarms can restore execution.**

- **The system resumes from reset**, not from the point it left off.

This mode consumes very little current—typically under 1 μA.

It's useful for:

- Devices that operate intermittently (e.g., once per hour)
- Wake-on-event systems
- Ultra-low-power sensors and loggers

To enter standby mode, you again set SLEEPDEEP and enable the standby bit in the power control registers (HAL-specific).

Example for STM32:

```
dp.PWR.cr.modify(|_, w| w.pdds().set_bit());
SCB::set_sleepdeep();
asm::wfi();
```

Keep in mind:

- RAM is lost—you need to persist state in backup SRAM or flash
- Peripherals are disabled
- You must reinitialize everything on wakeup

Summary Table (for Reference)

State	CPU	RAM	Clocks	Wake Sources	Current (typical)
Run	On	On	On	—	10–50 mA
Sleep	Off	On	Periph	Any interrupt	200–500 μA
Stop	Off	On	Off	RTC, EXTI, LPTIM	10–50 μA
Standby	Off	Off	Off	Wake pin, RTC alarm	<1 μA

These are not universal numbers—they vary by chip and settings. Always consult your microcontroller's datasheet and run measurements on real hardware using a current meter.

Practical Advice

- **Default to sleep mode** between tasks, even in simple firmware.

- **Use stop mode** for longer idle periods with minimal wake latency.
- **Use standby** when you're powered by coin cells, supercapacitors, or solar trickle charging and only need to wake occasionally.
- **Use event-driven architecture** (via interrupts or timers) instead of busy loops.
- **Avoid leaving peripherals running**—disable clocks, stop timers, and shut down ADC/DAC when not in use.

Exercise: Map Power Modes to Application Cases

1. Identify three real-world applications:
   - A GPS tracker with motion detection
   - A soil moisture sensor waking every 10 minutes
   - A remote control responding instantly to a button press
2. For each, decide:
   - Which sleep mode should be used?
   - What wake source is appropriate?
   - What needs to be re-initialized after wake?

Write out a brief firmware sketch showing your sleep/wake logic.

Understanding power states is essential for any firmware developer targeting embedded systems that need to live long, run cool, or work untethered. Fortunately, microcontrollers give you a fine degree of control, and Rust gives you the safety and structure to apply it reliably. The goal isn't to make firmware slower or less functional—but smarter, more responsive, and conscious of every microamp it consumes.

Configuring Low-Power Modes in Rust

Minimizing power usage in embedded systems isn't a matter of chance or compiler optimization—it's something you have to explicitly plan and implement. Thankfully, most modern microcontrollers, especially those built on ARM Cortex-M cores, come with a range of low-power modes that allow you to scale energy consumption depending on workload demand. These modes range from light sleep to complete system shutdown, and in Rust, configuring them is straightforward once you understand what registers need to be touched and what conditions must be met.

Preparing for Low-Power Configuration

Before you start issuing sleep commands, make sure you've:

- Disabled unused peripherals and clocks
- Configured appropriate wake-up sources (interrupts, RTC alarms, EXTI lines)
- Ensured the system clock can recover correctly after wake-up

Failing to prepare properly can lead to firmware freezes, missed wakeups, or corrupted peripheral states.

Sleep Mode (Light Sleep)

Sleep mode halts the CPU but leaves all peripherals and clocks running. It's useful when you just want to pause the main loop while waiting for an interrupt.

To enter sleep mode in Rust:

```rust
use cortex_m::asm::wfi;

loop {
    do_work();
    wfi(); // Enter sleep until an interrupt fires
}
```

This works out of the box on all Cortex-M devices, and no additional configuration is needed if you're using the default run-time behavior.

If you're using interrupts to trigger wake-ups—say, a button press or UART receive—you can safely sleep between events:

```rust
#[interrupt]
fn EXTI0() {
    log_info(&mut tx, "Woke up from EXTI0.");
    clear_interrupt_flag(); // Always clear the
source
}
```

The key here is: **wfi doesn't disable interrupts**—it just halts the CPU until the next one happens.

Stop Mode (Deep Sleep)

Stop mode provides much deeper savings than sleep, but it shuts off more of the chip—main system clocks are stopped. RAM is retained, but most peripherals halt.

You must configure two registers before calling `wfi`:

1. **System Control Block (SCB)**: to indicate that the CPU should enter deep sleep
2. **Power Control (PWR)**: to select stop mode (chip-specific)

Here's how you do that using STM32 PAC + HAL:

```
use cortex_m::peripheral::SCB;
use cortex_m::asm;
use stm32f4xx_hal::pac;

let dp = pac::Peripherals::take().unwrap();

// Enable deep sleep mode
SCB::set_sleepdeep();

// Optional: configure PWR register if needed
dp.PWR.cr.modify(|_, w| w.lpds().set_bit()); //
Low-power deep sleep

asm::wfi(); // Enter stop mode
```

This will halt the CPU and most of the chip, dropping current into the low microamp range. When an interrupt occurs (e.g., RTC, EXTI), the system resumes exactly where it left off.

You must be careful after waking:

- Reconfigure clocks if the system lost them during stop mode
- Re-enable peripheral clocks if required
- Double-check which interrupts are allowed to wake the chip in stop mode

Some HALs do this automatically; others require manual intervention.

Standby Mode (Full Shutdown with Wake on Reset)

Standby is the lowest power state. It cuts power to everything except a small part of the RTC domain and wake logic. RAM is lost, and execution resumes from reset.

In STM32, entering standby looks like this:

```
use cortex_m::peripheral::SCB;

dp.PWR.cr.modify(|_, w| w.pdds().set_bit()); //
Power-down deepsleep mode
SCB::set_sleepdeep();
asm::wfi(); // Enter standby
```

There's no return from standby—you start from scratch. So this mode is only suitable when:

- You need to sleep for hours or days
- You only need to wake on a button or RTC alarm
- You store persistent state in flash, EEPROM, or backup SRAM

After wake-up, you check the **standby flag** to determine the reset source.

HAL-Level Sleep API (Optional)

Some HALs (e.g., `nrf-hal`, `atsamd-hal`, and `esp-hal`) provide sleep abstractions directly:

```
let mut sleep = cortex_m::peripheral::SCB::borrow();
sleep.sleep(); // Regular WFI

sleep.deep_sleep(); // WFI with SLEEPDEEP
```

While these helpers are convenient, they often abstract away register configuration. For real control and observability, you should understand and configure SCB and PWR manually, as shown earlier.

Peripheral and Clock Management

Always shut down unused peripherals before sleeping. This is often done through the RCC peripheral (Reset and Clock Control):

```
dp.RCC.ahb1enr.modify(|_, w| w.gpioaen().clear_bit());
dp.RCC.apb1enr.modify(|_, w| w.tim2en().clear_bit());
```

Or with HAL methods:

```
let rcc = dp.RCC.constrain();
let clocks = rcc.cfgr.sysclk(8.mhz()).freeze(); //
Slow system clock
```

Dropping system frequency before sleeping gives you more time to finish tasks at lower energy cost.

Exercise: Dynamic Clock Scaling Before Sleep

1. Set up a main loop that reads a sensor every 1 second.
2. Before each reading, increase the system clock.
3. After the reading, reduce the clock and enter sleep.
4. Use a timer or RTC to wake periodically.

Measure current draw with a multimeter before and after adding these steps. You'll see dramatic differences.

Configuring low-power modes isn't about just putting the chip to sleep—it's about maintaining control and predictability as the system transitions across different power states. Rust doesn't abstract away this responsibility; instead, it gives you the tools to manage it precisely. With safe access to low-level registers, and a disciplined model of concurrency and side-effects, you can build systems that stay responsive while consuming just a few microamps between bursts of activity. That's the kind of control that turns a working firmware into a professional one.

Sleep/Wake Mechanisms and Wake Sources

Putting a microcontroller to sleep is only half the job. The real challenge—and where many firmware developers get tripped up—is waking it up correctly. Whether you're using a light sleep or deep standby mode, you need to be absolutely clear on *what* can wake the system, *when* it will do so, and *how* to structure your firmware so that the transition is seamless.

The microcontroller doesn't just magically resume from sleep. It wakes when one of the following events occurs:

- A **hardware interrupt** from a peripheral
- An **external pin change** (e.g., a button press)

- A **timer overflow or alarm** (e.g., RTC or SysTick)
- A **software interrupt**, triggered by another core or thread (less common in bare-metal)
- A **power management event**, such as USB resume or watchdog timeout

The type of sleep mode you're in determines which of these events can wake the chip.

Wake Source	Sleep	Stop	Standby
GPIO interrupt	✓	✓	✓ (via EXTI)
RTC alarm	✓	✓	✓
UART receive	✓	Some	✗
Timer overflow	✓	✓	✗
Software interrupt	✓	✓	✗

For example, standby mode can only be woken by events wired into the wakeup logic—typically EXTI lines or RTC alarms.

Setting Up Wake Sources in Rust

Let's walk through how to configure a few common wake sources using `stm32f4xx-hal` as our baseline.

1. Wake from External Interrupt (e.g., Button Press)

Suppose you want to wake the MCU when a button connected to PA0 is pressed.

Configure the GPIO pin:

```
let gpioa = dp.GPIOA.split();
let button = gpioa.pa0.into_pull_up_input();
```

Enable the EXTI interrupt line:

```
use stm32f4xx_hal::exti::{Exti, TriggerEdge};
```

```
let mut syscfg = dp.SYSCFG.constrain();
let mut exti = dp.EXTI;

button.make_interrupt_source(&mut syscfg);
button.trigger_on_edge(&mut exti,
TriggerEdge::Falling);
button.enable_interrupt(&mut exti);
```

Then, implement the interrupt handler:

```
#[interrupt]
fn EXTI0() {
    log_info(&mut tx, "Woke from EXTI0 (button
press)");
    clear_interrupt_flag(); // Always clear or EXTI
won't retrigger
}
```

Put the chip to sleep:

```
use cortex_m::asm;
asm::wfi(); // Wait For Interrupt
```

Now the chip sleeps until the button is pressed.

2. Wake from Timer (e.g., Every 1 Second)

You can use the Real-Time Clock (RTC) or a low-power timer to generate periodic wakeups.

Configure the RTC:

```
let mut rtc = Rtc::rtc(dp.RTC, &mut rcc.apb1, &mut
backup_domain);
rtc.enable_wakeup(RtcWakeup::Every1s);
```

Then enable the RTC interrupt:

```
rtc.listen_wakeup();
```

And define the handler:

```
#[interrupt]
fn RTC_WKUP() {
    log_info(&mut tx, "Woke up from RTC.");
    rtc.clear_wakeup_flag();
}
```

The chip will now wake every 1 second. Use this to do periodic tasks like sensor reads or data uploads.

Wake Behavior by Mode

Let's clarify how wake works in each sleep mode.

Sleep Mode

This is the easiest case. Any **enabled interrupt** can wake the CPU.

- You can sleep with `asm::wfi()`
- Your peripherals keep running
- Wakeup is near-instant
- No reinitialization needed

You typically use sleep mode for short idle periods between work chunks.

Stop Mode

In stop mode:

- Most clocks are off
- RAM is retained
- Peripherals may be halted
- Wake is triggered only by **selected interrupts** (e.g., RTC, EXTI)

After waking, you often need to:

- Re-enable system clocks
- Re-initialize peripherals
- Restore previous configuration (if not retained)

You enter stop mode with:

```
use cortex_m::peripheral::SCB;
```

```
SCB::set_sleepdeep();
asm::wfi();
```

Make sure the power control registers are also set appropriately (chip-specific).

Standby Mode

This is the lowest power state. Only wake sources routed to the power domain (like EXTI or RTC alarm) can bring it back.

On wake:

- MCU resets completely
- RAM is lost
- Program starts from `reset()` like a power-on boot

You must check flags to detect a wake-from-standby event, and reload state from persistent memory (if needed).

Software Wake-Up: Forcing an Interrupt

You can trigger a wake from software:

```
NVIC::pend(Interrupt::EXTI0); // Simulates EXTI0
interrupt
```

This is useful for testing or waking from an RTOS task or background process.

You can also set the interrupt manually on debug hardware to simulate events.

Exercise: Build a Multi-Source Wakeup System

1. Configure EXTI0 to trigger on button press.
2. Configure RTC to trigger every 5 seconds.
3. Enter stop mode using `sleepdeep()`.
4. In each ISR, log the wake source to UART.
5. Return to stop mode after handling each event.

This exercise teaches you to differentiate and handle wake sources properly, while keeping your firmware low-power and reactive.

Wake-up events are not just interrupts—they are *control signals* that bring your entire system back to life. If you configure them correctly, your firmware can sleep most of the time, wake up at the right moment, do its job quickly, and go right back to sleep. This rhythm is what makes modern embedded systems so efficient—and with Rust, you can handle it with confidence, precision, and the safety that only a systems language can offer.

Balancing Performance and Efficiency

In embedded systems, the goal is rarely just to be fast—it's to be *fast enough* while consuming the *least amount of energy possible*. This principle guides the architecture of energy-aware firmware: your code should wake up, do only what's needed, and return to sleep quickly, minimizing the time spent in high-power states. But striking this balance is more nuanced than it sounds, especially in systems that must respond quickly to external events, communicate over serial interfaces, or run periodic tasks with varying workloads.

Every decision in your firmware has an energy cost. Using a faster clock finishes tasks quicker but increases instantaneous current draw. Running at a lower frequency saves energy per second but may increase total energy per task if it takes longer. The trick is to consider both **energy per operation** and **idle energy cost**.

Let's clarify that with an example:

- Running at 84 MHz consumes 20 mA and completes a task in 10 ms.
- Running at 16 MHz consumes 5 mA but takes 60 ms for the same task.

Which is better?

- High-speed: 20 mA × 10 ms = 200 mA·ms
- Low-speed: 5 mA × 60 ms = 300 mA·ms

The faster version is more energy-efficient—even though it consumes more current, it finishes sooner and lets the CPU sleep longer.

So, **performance and efficiency are not opposites**—they can complement each other, if used wisely.

Dynamic Clock Scaling in Rust

One way to optimize power is to scale the system clock frequency based on workload.

With STM32 HAL:

```
let rcc = dp.RCC.constrain();
let clocks = rcc.cfgr.sysclk(8.mhz()).freeze();
```

If your MCU supports it, you can even reconfigure the clocks at runtime:

```
// Reduce clock before sleep
let clocks = rcc.cfgr.sysclk(4.mhz()).freeze();

// Increase clock for heavy task
let clocks = rcc.cfgr.sysclk(48.mhz()).freeze();
```

Keep in mind:

- Some peripherals (e.g., USB, SPI, PLLs) require minimum clock speeds.
- You may need to re-initialize peripherals that depend on the changed clock.

Use this technique when your workload fluctuates—like a sensor that samples slowly most of the time but occasionally transmits over radio.

Task Scheduling: Doing More with Less

When your firmware is structured around events or periodic tasks, try to **batch work** together. This reduces wakeups, peripheral toggling, and power transitions.

Here's how you might structure a system that reads a sensor every second and logs once per minute:

```
loop {
    if timer.has_elapsed_1s() {
```

```
        read_sensor();
    }

    if timer.has_elapsed_60s() {
        transmit_log();
    }

    sleep(); // wfi()
}
```

Each task is evaluated *only* when needed, and you spend as much time sleeping as possible. Grouping actions into bursts ensures the CPU remains active only when truly necessary.

Peripheral Gating and Clock Control

Disabling unused peripherals is one of the easiest wins for power savings. Most MCUs allow you to turn off clocks to GPIO blocks, timers, and even ADC/DAC modules.

In STM32:

```
dp.RCC.ahb1enr.modify(|_, w|
w.gpioaen().clear_bit());
```

If you're using a HAL:

```
let gpio = dp.GPIOA.split(); // Enables on use
drop(gpio); // Dropping disables (if HAL supports
this)
```

Disable peripherals immediately after use. For example, don't keep the ADC on if you only sample once per minute.

Also remember to turn off debugging (SWD/JTAG), as it often prevents deep sleep modes:

```
let mut dbg = dp.DBGMCU;
dbg.cr.modify(|_, w| w.dbg_sleep().clear_bit());
```

Monitoring and Adjusting in Real-Time

Efficient firmware isn't a "write once, done forever" process. You must **measure**, **tune**, and **adapt** based on actual performance and energy usage.

Use tools like:

- **Joulescope** or **Otii Arc** to measure current dynamically
- **STM32CubeMonitor** for current consumption graphs
- **Onboard current sense** peripherals, if supported

Example: if you notice that the system never enters stop mode due to a high-priority timer or ISR blocking the path to `wfi()`, restructure your interrupt logic.

Also, periodically reassess wakeup intervals. Many applications don't need precise timing—being off by a few milliseconds won't matter. Increase sleep duration or add jitter to reduce radio collisions and save energy.

Exercise: Energy-Aware LED Pattern

Write a program that:

1. Blinks an LED every second when in "active" mode.
2. Drops to sleep mode when no button is pressed for 30 seconds.
3. In sleep mode, only wakes every 5 seconds to blink once.
4. Restarts active blinking if the button is pressed.

You'll need:

- A timer (SysTick or RTC)
- A state machine to track activity
- `wfi()` to reduce power in idle periods

This teaches you how to shape system behavior around energy constraints without losing interactivity.

Balancing performance and efficiency is about making the microcontroller work just enough—no more, no less. In Embedded Rust, you can structure your system in such a way that the firmware runs quickly, sleeps deeply, and responds just in time. There's no need to overspend power just to "stay ready." With event-driven architecture, smart clock control, and clear sleep transitions, you can write firmware that's fast, responsive, and frugal—all at once.

Chapter 9: Structuring and Scaling Your Firmware

Once your embedded firmware starts to grow beyond a few peripheral setups and a main loop, code organization becomes just as important as correctness. It's one thing to blink an LED and read a sensor. It's another to support multiple sensors, manage communication interfaces, keep your logic testable, and eventually port the code to another microcontroller family altogether. That's where structure—clear, modular, idiomatic Rust structure—becomes your greatest asset.

Rust's type system and trait-based abstraction model make it especially well-suited for embedded firmware that needs to scale cleanly, stay maintainable, and remain portable across platforms. In this chapter, we'll unpack how to write firmware that's not only functional but also elegant, reusable, and robust—whether you're targeting a single board or an entire fleet of embedded devices.

Abstractions and Modularity with Traits

In embedded development, it's easy to fall into the trap of writing firmware that's too specific—hardwired to a particular board, sensor, or microcontroller. This works fine in small projects or one-off prototypes, but when your firmware grows or needs to support multiple platforms or configurations, that tight coupling quickly becomes a liability.

Rust offers an elegant, high-performance solution to this: **traits**. Traits let you define *what* something does without tying your code to *how* it does it. By using traits to describe capabilities—like reading a temperature, writing to storage, toggling an LED—you create a system that's modular, testable, and highly reusable. More importantly, your core logic becomes decoupled from the underlying hardware.

Embedded systems are full of side-effects: reading from sensors, toggling pins, talking to memory over SPI. If you write everything inline in `main.rs` using concrete types from your HAL or PAC, every part of your code knows about every other part. That's the opposite of scalable.

Traits solve this by giving you a way to define clear boundaries between logic and hardware. They enable:

- Pluggable components that work across devices
- Unit tests that don't touch real hardware
- Code that's easier to reason about and extend

In embedded contexts, think of traits as contracts for behaviors—like a temperature sensor or flash memory—not just abstract interfaces.

Writing Your First Embedded Trait

Say you're working with a temperature sensor. Instead of calling it directly from your main loop, define a trait:

```
pub trait TemperatureSensor {
    fn read_temperature(&mut self) -> Result<f32,
SensorError>;
}
```

This trait can now be implemented by any hardware driver. For example, the TMP102 sensor:

```
pub struct Tmp102<I2C> {
    i2c: I2C,
    address: u8,
}

impl<I2C, E> TemperatureSensor for Tmp102<I2C>
where
    I2C:
embedded_hal::blocking::i2c::WriteRead<Error = E> +
embedded_hal::blocking::i2c::Write<Error = E>,
{
    fn read_temperature(&mut self) -> Result<f32,
SensorError> {
        let mut buffer = [0u8; 2];
        self.i2c.write_read(self.address, &[0x00],
&mut buffer)?;

        let raw = ((buffer[0] as u16) << 4) |
((buffer[1] as u16) >> 4);
```

```
        Ok(raw as f32 * 0.0625)
    }
}
```

Now, in your application logic, you don't need to know *what* sensor is behind the reading—only that it satisfies `TemperatureSensor`.

Using Traits in Application Logic

Let's say you want to log a temperature every 5 seconds. You can write your application to depend on the trait:

```
pub struct Logger<S: TemperatureSensor> {
    sensor: S,
}

impl<S: TemperatureSensor> Logger<S> {
    pub fn poll(&mut self) {
        match self.sensor.read_temperature() {
            Ok(temp) => {
                log_info(&mut TX,
&format_args!("Temperature: {:.2} °C", temp));
            }
            Err(e) => {
                log_error(&mut TX, "Sensor read
failed");
            }
        }
    }
}
```

Notice that `Logger` doesn't care which sensor it's using. You can plug in a TMP102, an LM75, a fake sensor for testing, or even a simulator that generates sinusoidal values.

Mocking with Traits

Let's test this logger. You'll implement a mock sensor that satisfies the same trait:

```
pub struct MockSensor {
    value: f32,
```

```
}

impl TemperatureSensor for MockSensor {
    fn read_temperature(&mut self) -> Result<f32,
SensorError> {
        Ok(self.value)
    }
}
```

Now you can write a test:

```
#[test]
fn test_logging() {
    let sensor = MockSensor { value: 25.0 };
    let mut logger = Logger { sensor };

    logger.poll(); // Should log "Temperature:
25.00 °C"
}
```

No hardware involved. This is possible *only* because the behavior is abstracted behind a trait.

More Complex Traits: Storage and Display

You can layer multiple traits together to build complex applications. For example, a trait for logging to flash:

```
pub trait Storage {
    fn write_log(&mut self, value: f32) ->
Result<(), StorageError>;
}
```

And for a display:

```
pub trait Display {
    fn show_text(&mut self, text: &str);
}
```

Your app might now look like this:

```
pub struct App<S, F, D>
```

```
where
    S: TemperatureSensor,
    F: Storage,
    D: Display,
{
    sensor: S,
    flash: F,
    display: D,
}

impl<S, F, D> App<S, F, D>
where
    S: TemperatureSensor,
    F: Storage,
    D: Display,
{
    pub fn run(&mut self) {
        if let Ok(temp) =
self.sensor.read_temperature() {
            self.flash.write_log(temp).ok();
            self.display.show_text(&format!("Temp:
{:.2}°C", temp));
        }
    }
}
```

Now everything is modular, testable, and swappable. You've gone from bare-metal logic to a cleanly abstracted embedded application.

Exercise: Abstract a Buzzer Device

1. Define a trait `Buzzer` with `fn beep(&mut self, duration_ms: u32)`.
2. Implement it for a GPIO pin (using a HAL delay).
3. Create a `Notifier<B: Buzzer>` that emits a short beep on demand.
4. Create a `MockBuzzer` that logs to console.
5. Write a test that confirms the notifier calls `beep()` as expected.

This teaches you how to abstract actions with timing or side effects—very common in real systems.

Traits in embedded Rust aren't just a language feature—they're a design pattern for scalable firmware. They let you isolate logic from hardware, test behavior without a physical board, and build systems that adapt to change without major rewrites. If you structure your code this way from the beginning, you'll find that supporting new devices, adding features, or onboarding other developers becomes easier and faster. And your firmware becomes more than just code that works—it becomes code that lasts.

Organizing Code for Reusability

In embedded systems, one of the biggest challenges isn't blinking an LED or polling a sensor—it's managing the codebase once your project grows past the prototype phase. If everything lives in `main.rs`, and every peripheral is configured inline with your business logic, the firmware quickly becomes unmanageable. You can't test anything in isolation, reuse code across boards, or even understand what's going on without scrolling through hundreds of lines of tightly-coupled logic.

To avoid this, you need to structure your firmware for **reusability** from the start. That means clearly separating concerns, encapsulating logic, isolating hardware-specific code, and writing against interfaces rather than implementations. In Rust, the combination of strong typing, traits, and idiomatic module structure gives you the exact tools you need to build clean, maintainable firmware that's easy to scale and reuse.

In embedded systems, firmware often evolves in one of two ways:

1. It starts small and stays manageable… until one new feature breaks everything.
2. It starts messy and becomes impossible to test, port, or reason about.

The key to avoiding both is writing with *reuse* in mind—not just reuse of drivers or structs, but reuse of ideas and responsibilities. A well-structured codebase makes it easy to:

- Swap components without touching application logic
- Port firmware across boards or MCUs
- Write tests without physical hardware
- Add features without fear of breaking unrelated parts

Let's now look at how to structure your Rust embedded firmware to meet these goals.

Code Layout: High-Level Structure

Start by splitting your project into functional areas:

```
src/
├── main.rs
├── app/                    ← Application logic (business
rules, state)
│       ├── mod.rs
│       ├── logger.rs
│       └── state.rs
├── drivers/            ← Sensor and peripheral drivers
│       ├── mod.rs
│       ├── tmp102.rs
│       └── eeprom.rs
├── platform/               ← Board-specific setup and
configuration
│       ├── mod.rs
│       ├── clocks.rs
│       └── pinmap.rs
├── traits/              ← Shared capability traits
│       ├── mod.rs
│       └── temperature.rs
```

Each module has a clear purpose:

- `main.rs` bootstraps the system and ties everything together.
- `app/` holds logic that drives your product: polling sensors, processing inputs, deciding when to transmit.
- `drivers/` encapsulates hardware interactions, hidden behind `embedded-hal` traits.
- `platform/` maps out your MCU-specific pins and clock setup.
- `traits/` contains the contracts your drivers and app logic are built on.

This structure lets you evolve parts of your firmware independently.

Encapsulating Initialization

Board setup is often the messiest part of embedded Rust. Don't let it leak into your app logic.

In `platform/mod.rs`:

```rust
pub struct Board {
    pub i2c: I2C1,
    pub uart: Tx<UART2>,
    pub sensor: Tmp102<I2C1>,
}

pub fn init(dp: pac::Peripherals, cp:
pac::CorePeripherals) -> Board {
    let rcc = dp.RCC.constrain();
    let clocks =
rcc.cfgr.sysclk(48.mhz()).freeze();

    let gpiob = dp.GPIOB.split();
    let scl =
gpiob.pb8.into_alternate_open_drain();
    let sda =
gpiob.pb9.into_alternate_open_drain();
    let i2c = I2c::new(dp.I2C1, (scl, sda),
100.khz(), clocks);

    let sensor = Tmp102::new(i2c, 0x48);

    Board { i2c, sensor, uart }
}
```

This way, your `main.rs` stays clean:

```rust
fn main() -> ! {
    let dp = pac::Peripherals::take().unwrap();
    let cp = pac::CorePeripherals::take().unwrap();
    let mut board = platform::init(dp, cp);

    app::run(board);
}
```

Now if you change microcontrollers, you update only `platform.rs`, not your entire firmware.

Decoupling with Traits

Let's say your application needs to read temperature and store it. Write it generically:

```rust
use crate::traits::{TemperatureSensor, Storage};

pub struct Logger<T: TemperatureSensor, S: Storage>
{
    sensor: T,
    storage: S,
}

impl<T, S> Logger<T, S>
where
    T: TemperatureSensor,
    S: Storage,
{
    pub fn poll(&mut self) {
        if let Ok(temp) =
self.sensor.read_temperature() {
            self.storage.append_log(temp);
        }
    }
}
```

Neither the logger nor the application knows or cares about the exact sensor or storage implementation. That's the secret to scalable code: **depend on behavior, not implementation.**

Example Driver Layout

Your drivers should live in `drivers/` and follow this convention:

```rust
// drivers/tmp102.rs

use embedded_hal::blocking::i2c::{WriteRead,
Write};
use crate::traits::TemperatureSensor;

pub struct Tmp102<I2C> {
    i2c: I2C,
```

```
    addr: u8,
}

impl<I2C, E> TemperatureSensor for Tmp102<I2C>
where
    I2C: WriteRead<Error = E> + Write<Error = E>,
{
    fn read_temperature(&mut self) -> Result<f32,
SensorError> {
        let mut buf = [0u8; 2];
        self.i2c.write_read(self.addr, &[0x00],
&mut buf)?;
        let raw = ((buf[0] as u16) << 4) | ((buf[1]
as u16) >> 4);
        Ok(raw as f32 * 0.0625)
    }
}
```

You can now reuse `Tmp102` on any board that supplies an I2C bus. And you can test it with a mock I2C interface.

Reuse Across Boards or Products

When you write your logic and drivers against shared traits and isolate board setup in `platform/`, you can support multiple targets by creating different `platform/` implementations.

Example:

```
src/
├── platform_stm32/
├── platform_nrf52/
├── platform_simulator/
```

Each defines the same `Board` interface and initializes the correct hardware for that platform. Your application logic remains unchanged.

This makes your firmware portable by design.

Exercise: Restructure a Flat Firmware Project

1. Take an embedded project with logic in `main.rs`.

2. Move drivers to `drivers/`, app logic to `app/`, and board setup to `platform/`.
3. Define traits in `traits/` to abstract drivers.
4. Replace hardware types in the app with trait objects or generics.
5. Add a `MockSensor` and test the app without hardware.

You'll see instantly how much easier it becomes to read, test, and extend the code.

Good firmware isn't just about making peripherals work. It's about making *everything* work together: drivers, logic, tests, and portability. When your code is structured with clear boundaries—between hardware and logic, between platform and application—you make reuse the default, not the exception. And in embedded Rust, organizing for reusability means writing less boilerplate, writing fewer tests for the same behavior, and writing firmware you can actually enjoy maintaining.

Building Platform-Agnostic Drivers

In embedded development, the ability to reuse a hardware driver across multiple microcontrollers, boards, or projects is a massive advantage. Yet many drivers in embedded C are riddled with platform-specific logic—register names, peripheral initializations, or memory-mapped addresses—which makes them brittle and difficult to move to new hardware. Rust, by design, pushes you toward cleaner interfaces and encourages writing drivers that are *platform-agnostic*.

When a driver is platform-agnostic, it doesn't depend on any specific microcontroller, board, or peripheral implementation. It works with any hardware that can satisfy a small set of clearly defined behaviors. In Rust, this is achieved using traits from the `embedded-hal` crate—an ecosystem-wide abstraction layer for embedded hardware capabilities.

Start with Traits, Not Types

The foundation of portability is abstraction. You don't want to talk to a specific I2C peripheral—you want to talk to something that *can write and read bytes over I2C*. That's what `embedded-hal` provides.

Here's an I2C trait example from `embedded-hal`:

```
pub trait WriteRead {
    type Error;
    fn write_read(
        &mut self,
        addr: u8,
        bytes: &[u8],
        buffer: &mut [u8],
    ) -> Result<(), Self::Error>;
}
```

That's all a driver needs to depend on: this behavior.

Example: A Reusable I2C Temperature Sensor Driver

Suppose you're writing a driver for the TMP102 digital temperature sensor. It
talks over I2C using a 7-bit address and returns a 12-bit temperature value.

Start by defining your driver:

```
use embedded_hal::blocking::i2c::{Write,
WriteRead};

pub struct Tmp102<I2C> {
    i2c: I2C,
    address: u8,
}

impl<I2C, E> Tmp102<I2C>
where
    I2C: Write<Error = E> + WriteRead<Error = E>,
{
    pub fn new(i2c: I2C, address: u8) -> Self {
        Self { i2c, address }
    }

    pub fn read_temperature(&mut self) ->
Result<f32, E> {
        let mut buf = [0u8; 2];
        self.i2c.write_read(self.address, &[0x00],
&mut buf)?;
```

```rust
        let raw = ((buf[0] as u16) << 4) | ((buf[1]
as u16) >> 4);
        let temp_celsius = raw as f32 * 0.0625;
        Ok(temp_celsius)
    }

    pub fn release(self) -> I2C {
        self.i2c
    }
}
```

This driver doesn't depend on any MCU, register block, or HAL. It only requires an I2C interface that conforms to `embedded-hal`. As long as the user passes in a compliant I2C instance, the driver works.

Using the Driver on STM32

On an STM32F4, your HAL might give you this:

```rust
let i2c = I2c::new(
    dp.I2C1,
    (scl, sda),
    100.khz(),
    clocks,
);
let mut sensor = Tmp102::new(i2c, 0x48);
```

Now the exact same driver could be reused on RP2040, nRF52, or even in a PC simulation using mocks. It doesn't care—it only cares about the trait.

Supporting SPI Devices: Flash Driver Example

Here's a reusable SPI flash driver for a chip like the W25Q32:

```rust
use embedded_hal::blocking::spi::Transfer;
use embedded_hal::digital::v2::OutputPin;

pub struct Flash<SPI, CS> {
    spi: SPI,
    cs: CS,
}
```

```
impl<SPI, CS, E> Flash<SPI, CS>
where
    SPI: Transfer<u8, Error = E>,
    CS: OutputPin,
{
    pub fn read_id(&mut self) -> Result<[u8; 3], E>
    {
        let mut buf = [0x9F, 0, 0, 0];

        self.cs.set_low().ok();
        self.spi.transfer(&mut buf)?;
        self.cs.set_high().ok();

        Ok([buf[1], buf[2], buf[3]])
    }

    pub fn release(self) -> (SPI, CS) {
        (self.spi, self.cs)
    }
}
```

Once again, there's no dependency on `stm32f4xx-hal`, `nrf-hal`, or any specific board crate. The only requirement is that the passed-in SPI and CS types implement the expected traits.

Abstracting Complex Devices

For more complex drivers—such as displays, sensor fusion modules, or motor controllers—your public API may expose more functions, and your internal logic may maintain state. But your dependency model should remain the same:

- Use HAL traits only
- Encapsulate all logic behind public methods
- Keep transport (I2C/SPI) and interface (commands, parsing) tightly scoped

For example, a driver for an IMU sensor might expose:

```
impl<I2C, E> Mpu6050<I2C>
where
    I2C: Write + WriteRead,
{
```

```
    pub fn init(&mut self) -> Result<(), E> { ... }
    pub fn read_accel(&mut self) -> Result<[f32;
3], E> { ... }
    pub fn read_gyro(&mut self) -> Result<[f32; 3],
E> { ... }
}
```

With all bus interaction hidden, users only interact with sensor logic.

Testing with `embedded-hal-mock`

To ensure your driver behaves correctly, test it with mocks:

```
use embedded_hal_mock::i2c::{Mock as I2cMock,
Transaction as I2cTransaction};

#[test]
fn test_read_temperature() {
    let expectations = [
        I2cTransaction::write_read(0x48,
vec![0x00], vec![0x1A, 0x00]),
    ];
    let mock = I2cMock::new(&expectations);

    let mut sensor = Tmp102::new(mock, 0x48);
    let temp = sensor.read_temperature().unwrap();
    assert!((temp - 26.0).abs() < 0.1);
}
```

This kind of test would be impossible with platform-bound logic. But with trait-bound, platform-free drivers, you can simulate sensor behavior, test conversions, and validate fallbacks easily.

Exercise: Write and Test a Reusable LED Driver

1. Define a struct `StatusLed<PIN>` where `PIN: OutputPin`.
2. Implement `fn on()`, `fn off()`, and `fn toggle()` methods.
3. Implement a mock using `embedded-hal-mock::pin::Mock`.
4. Write a unit test that verifies the LED turns on and off as expected.

This exercise reinforces writing against interfaces, not implementations, and validates behavior without relying on a physical LED.

Reusable drivers are one of the clearest benefits of Embedded Rust. When you depend only on `embedded-hal` traits, your drivers become portable, testable, and production-ready from day one. Whether you're building firmware for a custom PCB, a dev kit, or a simulated lab environment, platform-agnostic drivers let you focus on what matters—behavior, correctness, and reliability. And once you adopt this style, you'll never want to write MCU-bound firmware again.

Testing and Mocking Hardware Behavior

In embedded development, the smallest bug in hardware communication can result in catastrophic failure—misreading a sensor, corrupting flash, or silently missing a critical interrupt. Yet, unlike desktop software, embedded code has to work with physical constraints: there's no standard operating system, the hardware isn't always available during development, and reproducing a bug in the field can be a nightmare. That's where testing and mocking come in.

With Rust, you're not left guessing. The language enforces correctness through type safety, but more importantly, it lets you design systems that are testable even *without* access to the real hardware. If you write your firmware using traits and abstractions, as we covered in the last sections, then testing becomes not just possible, but practical and reliable.

Designing for Testability

The first rule of testable embedded firmware is: **decouple logic from hardware**.

Don't write application logic directly against `stm32f4xx_hal::I2c1` or `rcc.cfgr.sysclk(...)`. Instead, wrap hardware interaction in traits and pass them into your logic.

For example, instead of this:

```
let mut sensor = Tmp102::new(i2c, 0x48);
let temp = sensor.read_temperature().unwrap();
```

Write this:

```
pub trait TemperatureSensor {
```

```
    fn read_temperature(&mut self) -> Result<f32,
SensorError>;
}

pub struct Logger<S: TemperatureSensor> {
    sensor: S,
}

impl<S: TemperatureSensor> Logger<S> {
    pub fn log(&mut self) -> Result<(),
SensorError> {
        let temp = self.sensor.read_temperature()?;
        log_info(&mut TX, &format_args!("Temp:
{:.1}°C", temp));
        Ok(())
    }
}
```

Now your `Logger` works with *any* type that implements the `TemperatureSensor` trait—including mocks for testing.

Mocking with `embedded-hal-mock`

The `embedded-hal-mock` crate provides trait implementations that simulate I2C, SPI, GPIO, and more. You define a sequence of expected transactions, and the mock enforces them during tests.

Here's how to test a temperature sensor driver that reads from an I2C address:

```
# Cargo.toml (test dependencies)
[dev-dependencies]
embedded-hal-mock = "0.8"
```

Now the test:

```
use embedded_hal_mock::i2c::{Mock as I2cMock,
Transaction as I2cTransaction};

#[test]
fn reads_valid_temperature() {
    let expectations = [
```

```
        I2cTransaction::write_read(0x48,
vec![0x00], vec![0x1A, 0x00]), // Raw: 0x1A0
    ];
    let i2c = I2cMock::new(&expectations);

    let mut sensor = Tmp102::new(i2c, 0x48);
    let temp = sensor.read_temperature().unwrap();

    assert!((temp - 26.0).abs() < 0.1);
}
```

The mock enforces both the sequence and the data. If your driver writes or reads something unexpected, the test fails.

This way, you can write dozens of tests that verify every edge case without wiring a single sensor.

Mocking GPIO

Need to simulate an output pin, like a status LED or a CS line for SPI?

```
use embedded_hal_mock::pin::{Mock as PinMock, State
as PinState, Transaction as PinTransaction};

#[test]
fn toggles_led_correctly() {
    let expectations = [
            PinTransaction::set(PinState::High),
            PinTransaction::set(PinState::Low),
    ];

    let pin = PinMock::new(&expectations);
    let mut led = StatusLed::new(pin);

    led.on().unwrap();
    led.off().unwrap();
}
```

This validates that your code actually toggles the pin as expected.

You can also use this approach to test chip-select behavior in SPI drivers or interrupt flags.

Mocking Flash, Timers, and Sensors

For more complex peripherals like flash memory or timers, write your own mocks by implementing the required traits.

Example mock for a `Storage` trait:

```
pub struct MockStorage {
    pub log: Vec<f32>,
}

impl Storage for MockStorage {
    fn append_log(&mut self, value: f32) ->
Result<(), StorageError> {
        self.log.push(value);
        Ok(())
    }
}
```

This lets you inspect state after logic runs:

```
#[test]
fn logs_temperature_to_storage() {
    let sensor = MockSensor { value: 25.5 };
    let storage = MockStorage { log: vec![] };
    let mut logger = Logger { sensor, storage };

    logger.log().unwrap();
    assert_eq!(logger.storage.log, vec![25.5]);
}
```

This pattern scales well to queues, radio transmitters, or motor drivers.

Simulating Errors and Edge Cases

Mocks aren't just for happy paths. Use them to test failure conditions too:

```
pub struct FaultySensor;

impl TemperatureSensor for FaultySensor {
    fn read_temperature(&mut self) -> Result<f32,
SensorError> {
```

```
            Err(SensorError::NoAck)
    }
}

#[test]
fn handles_sensor_error_gracefully() {
    let sensor = FaultySensor;
    let storage = MockStorage { log: vec![] };
    let mut logger = Logger { sensor, storage };

    let result = logger.log();
    assert!(result.is_err());
}
```

This is where embedded Rust shines—because `Result` is enforced, you *have to* handle the error, and the compiler helps you make sure you do.

Integration Testing on Real Hardware

Once your drivers and logic are tested in isolation, run higher-level integration tests on the actual board:

- Use UART logging for visibility
- Toggle an LED to indicate state
- Capture behavior with logic analyzers or serial terminals

Even if your test is just:

```
loop {
    let temp = sensor.read_temperature().unwrap();
    writeln!(tx, "Temp: {:.2}", temp).unwrap();
    delay.delay_ms(1000u32);
}
```

That's a valuable smoke test to verify full-stack correctness—from init to peripheral to logic.

You can also combine hardware tests with CI by using probes like `probe-rs` to flash and reset boards during automated runs.

Exercise: End-to-End Test with a Mock Sensor

1. Define a `Sensor` trait with a `read()` method.
2. Implement `MockSensor` that returns a fixed or incrementing value.
3. Create a `Logger<S>` that logs each reading to a `Vec<f32>`.
4. Write a test that simulates five readings and asserts the final log.

This solidifies trait-based design, test-driven development, and mocking concepts in practice.

Testing embedded systems doesn't mean guessing or plugging in boards blindly. With the right design—traits for abstraction, mocks for simulation, and `Result`-based APIs for error capture—you can validate the most critical parts of your firmware *before* you ever flash a chip. And when you do flash, you already know the core logic is sound. That's the power of Embedded Rust—and it changes the way you approach firmware forever.

Chapter 10: Real-World Firmware Deployment

At this point, you've written structured, testable, and efficient embedded Rust code. You've abstracted your drivers, modularized your logic, and validated behavior with mocks and unit tests. But firmware isn't complete until it runs reliably on real hardware—and that's what this chapter is about.

Firmware deployment is the final bridge between code and product. It's where you connect your development workflow to physical microcontrollers, load your binaries into flash memory, and verify that everything performs as expected in the field. In Rust, this process is aided by powerful tooling— `probe-rs`, OpenOCD, GDB, and `defmt`—that gives you full control, rich diagnostics, and deep visibility into your code's runtime behavior.

Flashing Firmware with `probe-rs` and OpenOCD

At some point, you have to move beyond simulations and mocks. The firmware you've written—regardless of how well it's structured or tested— won't matter until it's running on actual hardware. That's where flashing comes in: transferring your compiled `.elf` or `.bin` file into the microcontroller's non-volatile memory so it can start executing the code you've built.

In the Rust embedded ecosystem, you typically use one of two tools for flashing: `probe-rs` or OpenOCD. Both are widely used, and each has its strengths. `probe-rs` is written in Rust and integrates tightly with the Rust tooling chain. OpenOCD is more established, highly configurable, and compatible with a wide variety of debug probes. Both give you access to the chip's SWD or JTAG interface, and both support flashing, memory inspection, and breakpoint-based debugging.

Before you flash anything, you should:

- Have a microcontroller connected via a debug probe (e.g., ST-Link, J-Link, CMSIS-DAP)
- Know your exact chip model (e.g., `STM32F401RETx`)

- Compile your firmware using the correct Rust target (e.g., `thumbv7em-none-eabihf`)
- Ensure that your probe is detected by the host machine (USB permissions, drivers, etc.)

You'll also want your Rust firmware in `release` mode, since this ensures all optimizations are applied and your binary is production-ready:

```
cargo build --release --target thumbv7em-none-eabihf
```

Once this is in place, you're ready to flash.

Flashing with `probe-rs`

Installation

To get started with `probe-rs`, install the CLI tools:

```
cargo install probe-rs-cli
cargo install cargo-flash
```

Basic Usage with `cargo-flash`

The easiest way to flash using `probe-rs` is through `cargo-flash`, which builds and flashes in one command:

```
cargo flash --chip STM32F401RETx --release
```

Replace `STM32F401RETx` with your actual chip name, which you can find in your datasheet or on the microcontroller itself.

This command will:

- Automatically detect your connected probe
- Build your project if needed
- Flash the compiled binary to the microcontroller
- Reset the MCU afterward (unless you pass `--disable-reset`)

Advanced: Flashing with `probe-rs-cli`

For more control, you can use the lower-level `probe-rs-cli` tool:

```
probe-rs-cli list
```

This shows connected probes. Then:

```
probe-rs-cli run --chip STM32F401RETx
./target/thumbv7em-none-eabihf/release/app
```

This bypasses `cargo` and flashes a specific binary directly.

You can also erase flash before writing:

```
probe-rs-cli erase --chip STM32F401RETx
```

Or read memory regions for debugging:

```
probe-rs-cli read-memory --chip STM32F401RETx --
address 0x2000_0000 --length 64
```

Troubleshooting Tips

- If the device isn't detected, check USB permissions and kernel drivers (especially on Linux).
- Use a powered USB hub if your probe draws more current than the host provides.
- Double-check that the target chip ID matches your board.

Flashing with OpenOCD

OpenOCD (Open On-Chip Debugger) is a long-standing tool that works with dozens of chips and probes.

Installation

Install with your package manager:

- macOS: `brew install open-ocd`
- Ubuntu/Debian: `sudo apt install openocd`

You'll also need the ARM toolchain:

```
sudo apt install gcc-arm-none-eabi gdb-multiarch
```

Configuring OpenOCD

You need to specify two things:

- **Interface configuration** (e.g., `stlink.cfg`, `cmsis-dap.cfg`)
- **Target configuration** (e.g., `stm32f4x.cfg`, `nrf52.cfg`)

Start OpenOCD:

```
openocd -f interface/stlink.cfg -f
target/stm32f4x.cfg
```

You'll see output like:

```
Info : clock speed 1000 kHz
Info : STLINK v2 JTAG v30 API v2 SWIM v25 VID
0x0483 PID 0x3748
Info : stm32f4x.cpu: hardware has 6 breakpoints, 4
watchpoints
```

This opens a GDB server on port 3333.

Flashing with GDB

Compile your firmware:

```
cargo build --release --target thumbv7em-none-
eabihf
```

Start GDB:

```
arm-none-eabi-gdb target/thumbv7em-none-
eabihf/release/app
```

Then connect to OpenOCD:

```
(gdb) target remote :3333
(gdb) monitor reset halt
(gdb) load
(gdb) monitor reset run
```

```
(gdb) quit
```

This loads the binary into flash and starts execution.

Exercise: Flash a Blinking LED Firmware

1. Write a minimal LED blink example for your board.
2. Build it with `cargo build --release`.
3. Flash using both `cargo flash` and OpenOCD+GDB.
4. Measure and compare flashing time and reset behavior.

This exercise helps you validate the toolchain, confirm memory mapping, and inspect the end-to-end deployment process.

Flashing is the final gate between development and validation. With Rust tooling like `probe-rs` and traditional tools like OpenOCD, you have full control over how your firmware lands on hardware. And once you get comfortable with either workflow, deploying to real devices becomes just another step—fast, repeatable, and reliable.

Debugging with GDB and RTT

Writing firmware is only half the job. When something doesn't work— whether it's a missed interrupt, a corrupted value, or a hard fault—your ability to observe, pause, inspect, and reason through the code's behavior on real hardware becomes essential. In Embedded Rust, debugging isn't limited to blinking LEDs or UART print statements. With tools like GDB and RTT, you can go much deeper—interactively exploring memory, stepping through code, and logging messages directly from a running microcontroller with minimal performance overhead.

Setting the Stage: When You Need Real Debugging

There are situations where mock testing and code inspection fall short:

- You're getting a `HardFault` and don't know why.
- A peripheral works sometimes but not always.
- Your firmware crashes or hangs after several minutes.
- Data from a sensor appears valid, but changes erratically.

These are problems that only **runtime visibility** can solve—and that's where GDB and RTT shine.

Using GDB: Inspect, Step, and Break

GDB is a command-line debugger that supports setting breakpoints, stepping through code, examining registers, and inspecting memory. It connects to your running firmware via a debug probe and gives you low-level control over program execution.

Setting Up GDB

Make sure you have:

- The ARM Embedded GDB installed: `arm-none-eabi-gdb`
- A running GDB server (`OpenOCD` or `probe-rs`)
- A Rust binary built with debug info:

```
cargo build --target thumbv7em-none-eabihf
```

Start OpenOCD (example for STM32F4):

```
openocd -f interface/stlink.cfg -f
target/stm32f4x.cfg
```

Then in a second terminal:

```
arm-none-eabi-gdb target/thumbv7em-none-
eabihf/debug/app
```

In GDB:

```
target remote :3333
monitor reset halt
break main
continue
```

Now you can:

- Step line-by-line (`step`, `next`)
- Print variables (`print my_var`)
- Watch memory (`x/4xw 0x2000_0000`)

- Inspect registers (`info registers`)
- Get backtraces on crash (`backtrace`)

Example: Catching a HardFault

Suppose your firmware crashes when reading from a peripheral.

Start GDB and run:

```
target remote :3333
continue
```

The debugger pauses automatically on crash. You can now do:

```
backtrace
info registers
```

This tells you what function caused the fault, what values were in registers, and how far the stack reached. From here, you can trace back to the faulty access and fix the bug.

You can also place a breakpoint at the handler itself:

```
break HardFault
```

And examine the system state the moment it occurs.

Logging with RTT: Real-Time Insight Without `println!`

Standard `println!` doesn't work in `no_std` environments. You could use UART, but that requires configuring a serial port, dealing with baud rate issues, and losing valuable cycles during transmission.

RTT (Real-Time Transfer) solves this. It uses the debug interface to stream log messages from the MCU to your host in real time—without interrupting program execution.

Setting Up RTT with `defmt`

Add these dependencies:

```
[dependencies]
defmt = "0.3"
defmt-rtt = "0.3"
panic-probe = "0.3"

[features]
default = ["defmt-default"]
defmt-default = ["defmt", "defmt-rtt", "panic-
probe"]
In main.rs:
#[entry]
fn main() -> ! {
    defmt::info!("System initialized");
    loop {
        let temp = read_temperature();
        defmt::info!("Temperature: {:.2} °C",
temp);
        delay.delay_ms(1000);
    }
}
```

Then run:

```
cargo run --release
```

This command (provided by `probe-rs`) builds, flashes, and opens an RTT session automatically, printing logs as they arrive.

Benefits of defmt

- Very low overhead
- Compression for minimal log size
- Panic handling with full context
- Easy integration with `probe-run`

This makes it ideal for production firmware where you can't afford UART delay or want to log while sleeping or running real-time tasks.

Combining GDB and RTT

You can use both tools together: GDB for step-by-step debugging and RTT for streaming insight. For example:

- Use GDB to halt at a breakpoint.
- Watch logs in RTT while stepping.
- Resume and observe log output on a live system.

This hybrid approach gives you both **control** and **visibility**—something traditional embedded tools struggle to balance.

Exercise: Debug and Log a Faulty Sensor Driver

1. Write a driver for a fake sensor that sometimes returns an invalid reading.
2. Use `defmt::info!` to log each read.
3. Inject a panic when the reading is below a threshold.
4. Flash the firmware and run with RTT.
5. Open GDB, catch the panic, and inspect the sensor's internal state.

This teaches you to correlate logs with crashes and explore root causes interactively.

GDB and RTT don't replace testing—they complement it. They give you the ability to step into your firmware, ask it questions, and watch it answer them live. Whether you're chasing a crash, tuning performance, or verifying edge behavior, these tools will help you work faster, debug smarter, and ultimately build better firmware that's not just functional, but trustworthy. In Embedded Rust, they're not optional extras—they're essential parts of your development toolkit.

Optimizing for Size and Speed

Embedded firmware often lives under tight constraints. You may be working with 128 KB of flash, 16 KB of RAM, and clock speeds under 48 MHz. When every byte and cycle matters, optimization isn't about theoretical gains—it's a necessity. Whether you're deploying to a small Cortex-M0 or fitting more features into a larger M4, understanding how to fine-tune your Rust firmware for size and speed makes the difference between "barely runs" and "production-ready."

Rust offers powerful control over how code is compiled, linked, and executed. With careful profiling, smart configuration, and practical code hygiene, you can reduce your binary size, speed up execution paths, and ensure your firmware makes the most of its limited hardware.

Let's say your firmware is sitting at 120 KB out of a 128 KB flash budget. Now marketing wants you to add BLE, OTA updates, and a flash filesystem. Without optimization, your only option is to buy a bigger chip—which costs more, consumes more power, and forces a redesign.

Or consider a motor control loop that runs every 1 ms. If your math operations take 1.5 ms, you start missing deadlines. Miss enough, and your system becomes unstable.

Optimizing code means you can:

- Fit more features in limited memory
- Meet real-time deadlines
- Reduce power usage
- Avoid performance bottlenecks
- Increase battery life

Let's start with code size.

Reducing Firmware Size

Use `opt-level = "z"`

In your `Cargo.toml`, set your release profile to favor size over speed:

```
[profile.release]
opt-level = "z"    # Optimize for binary size
codegen-units = 1
lto = true         # Enable Link Time Optimization
panic = "abort"    # Don't include unwinding
machinery
```

This tells the compiler to aggressively reduce code size, even if that slightly slows execution.

Strip Unused Symbols with `objcopy`

Once built, use `objcopy` to strip your binary:

```
arm-none-eabi-objcopy -O binary target/thumbv7em-none-eabihf/release/app app.bin
```

Or inspect the ELF size:

```
arm-none-eabi-size -A target/thumbv7em-none-
eabihf/release/app
```

This shows the size of `.text` (code), `.rodata` (read-only data), and `.bss` (uninitialized static variables).

Avoid `core::fmt` Overhead

Avoid `format!`, `println!`, or any use of `core::fmt` in production builds. They pull in formatting machinery and inflate binary size. Instead, use fixed messages or use `defmt`, which compresses logs.

Replace this:

```
println!("Temperature: {}", temp);
```

With:

```
defmt::info!("Temp = {} C", temp); // Smaller and
efficient
```

Or remove logs entirely from release builds.

Analyzing with `cargo bloat`

To find what's bloating your firmware:

```
cargo install cargo-bloat
cargo bloat --release --target thumbv7em-none-
eabihf
```

This outputs the size of every function in your binary, ranked by contribution to total size.

Sample output:

```
File   .text      Size   Crate Name
0.0%   0.1%  1.6K   cortex-m-rt   __reset
1.4%   1.4%  2.4K   myapp         calculate_crc
8.5%   8.5%  5.7K   myapp         format_float
```

Now you can rewrite or replace bloated functions.

Cutting Costs: Panic Handling

The default panic handler adds bloat because it supports backtraces and formatting. In `Cargo.toml`:

```
[dependencies]
panic-halt = "0.2"

[profile.release]
panic = "abort"
```

Use it in `main.rs`:

```
use panic_halt as _; // Halts on panic
```

Now panics don't try to print anything—they just lock up, which is fine for production embedded systems.

Speeding Up Execution

Tune Critical Paths

If you have routines that run on a schedule—like sensor reads or control loops—optimize them specifically. Avoid floating-point math unless your chip has an FPU. Replace:

```
let angle = (steps as f32) * 1.8;
```

With:

```
let angle = (steps as u16) * 18 / 10; // Integer
math
```

Measure execution time with a GPIO pin:

```
led.set_high().ok();
do_work();
led.set_low().ok();
```

Then use a logic analyzer to measure time between toggles.

Profile with `perf`, ITM, or DWT

Use DWT cycle counters on Cortex-M for accurate cycle counting:

```
use cortex_m::peripheral::DWT;

let cycles_before = DWT::get_cycle_count();
do_work();
let cycles_after = DWT::get_cycle_count();
defmt::info!("Cycles: {}", cycles_after -
cycles_before);
```

Enable DWT:

```
DWT::unlock();
DWT::enable_cycle_counter();
```

This gives you direct insight into which paths take too long.

Disable Unused Features

Don't pull in unused traits or modules. In `Cargo.toml`:

```
[dependencies]
embedded-hal = { version = "1.0.0", features =
["spi"] } # not "full"
```

Use feature flags for your own crates:

```
[features]
default = ["sensor"]
sensor = []
ble = []
```

Then guard code:

```
#[cfg(feature = "sensor")]
fn read_sensor() { ... }
```

This lets you strip out unneeded code at compile time.

Exercise: Optimize a Logging System

1. Build a simple firmware that logs sensor data every second using `println!()`.
2. Measure firmware size with `cargo bloat`.
3. Replace `println!` with `defmt::info!` and re-measure.
4. Apply `opt-level = "z"` and `panic = "abort"`.
5. Compare resulting `.elf` and `.bin` sizes.

By the end, you'll have a logging system that's just as functional—but 50–80% smaller and faster.

In embedded systems, efficiency isn't about premature optimization—it's about making deliberate decisions based on real constraints. With Rust, you're not forced to trade performance for safety or readability. You get tight binaries, fast loops, and safe concurrency—all with modern tooling to guide your efforts. Whether you're squeezing into 32 KB or trying to hit a 1 ms deadline, the right optimizations make your firmware not just better—but possible.

Case Study: A Complete Sensor-Based Project

Theory is essential—but theory doesn't ship. In this final section, we bring everything together in a complete, real-world firmware project. You'll see how to build and deploy a temperature-logging system that runs on bare-metal Rust, talks to hardware using traits and drivers, logs data with RTT, sleeps to save power, and can be debugged and flashed reliably. This is a practical, production-ready example, structured exactly how you'd write real firmware—not for a tutorial, but for a product.

We'll walk step-by-step from project structure to final flashing, integrating concepts from all previous chapters: abstraction, driver reuse, power optimization, debugging, and testing. The entire system fits in under 32 KB and runs on affordable Cortex-M development boards like the STM32F401 or nRF52840.

Project Goal

Build a firmware that:

- Reads temperature from a TMP102 sensor over I2C

- Logs readings every 5 seconds using RTT and `defmt`
- Blinks an LED as a status heartbeat
- Sleeps between readings to minimize power consumption
- Handles sensor read errors gracefully

Target platform: STM32F401RE (Cortex-M4), using `probe-rs` and `defmt`.

1. Project Structure

Start with this folder layout:

```
src/
├── main.rs
├── app/
│   ├── mod.rs
│   ├── logger.rs
├── drivers/
│   ├── mod.rs
│   ├── tmp102.rs
├── platform/
│   ├── mod.rs
│   └── board.rs
├── traits/
│   └── temperature.rs
```

This layout separates concerns cleanly:

- `main.rs`: Boot and top-level orchestration
- `platform/`: Hardware initialization (I2C, GPIO, clocks)
- `traits/`: Sensor capabilities as abstract interfaces
- `drivers/`: Hardware-specific logic behind traits
- `app/`: High-level application logic

2. Defining the Temperature Sensor Trait

```
src/traits/temperature.rs:
pub trait TemperatureSensor {
    fn read_temperature(&mut self) -> Result<f32,
SensorError>;
}
```

```
#[derive(Debug)]
pub enum SensorError {
    Communication,
    InvalidReading,
}
```

This defines a contract. Any sensor that implements this trait can be plugged into the app logic.

3. Implementing the TMP102 Driver

```
src/drivers/tmp102.rs:
use embedded_hal::blocking::i2c::{Write,
WriteRead};
use crate::traits::temperature::{TemperatureSensor,
SensorError};

pub struct Tmp102<I2C> {
    i2c: I2C,
    addr: u8,
}

impl<I2C, E> Tmp102<I2C>
where
    I2C: Write + WriteRead<Error = E>,
{
    pub fn new(i2c: I2C, addr: u8) -> Self {
        Self { i2c, addr }
    }
}

impl<I2C, E> TemperatureSensor for Tmp102<I2C>
where
    I2C: Write + WriteRead<Error = E>,
{
    fn read_temperature(&mut self) -> Result<f32,
SensorError> {
        let mut buf = [0u8; 2];
        self.i2c.write_read(self.addr, &[0x00],
&mut buf)
```

```
        .map_err(|_|
SensorError::Communication)?;

        let raw = ((buf[0] as u16) << 4) | ((buf[1]
as u16) >> 4);
        Ok(raw as f32 * 0.0625)
    }
}
```

4. Logger Logic

src/app/logger.rs:

```
use crate::traits::temperature::TemperatureSensor;
use defmt::{info, warn};

pub struct Logger<S: TemperatureSensor> {
    sensor: S,
}

impl<S: TemperatureSensor> Logger<S> {
    pub fn new(sensor: S) -> Self {
        Self { sensor }
    }

    pub fn poll(&mut self) {
        match self.sensor.read_temperature() {
            Ok(temp) => info!("Temp: {:.2}°C",
temp),
            Err(_) => warn!("Sensor read failed"),
        }
    }
}
```

This logic is decoupled from hardware—it can be reused in tests or with different sensors.

5. Platform Setup

src/platform/board.rs:

```
use stm32f4xx_hal::{pac, prelude::*, i2c::I2c};
```

```rust
use embedded_hal::blocking::delay::DelayMs;
use cortex_m::peripheral::Peripherals as
CorePeripherals;
use crate::drivers::tmp102::Tmp102;

pub struct Board<I2C> {
    pub sensor: Tmp102<I2C>,
    pub delay: cortex_m::delay::Delay,
}

pub fn init() -> Board<impl
embedded_hal::blocking::i2c::WriteRead<Error = impl
core::fmt::Debug>> {
    let dp = pac::Peripherals::take().unwrap();
    let cp = CorePeripherals::take().unwrap();

    let rcc = dp.RCC.constrain();
    let clocks =
rcc.cfgr.sysclk(48.mhz()).freeze();

    let gpio = dp.GPIOB.split();
    let scl = gpio.pb8.into_alternate_open_drain();
    let sda = gpio.pb9.into_alternate_open_drain();

    let i2c = I2c::new(dp.I2C1, (scl, sda),
100.khz(), clocks);
    let delay =
cortex_m::delay::Delay::new(cp.SYST, clocks);

    let sensor = Tmp102::new(i2c, 0x48);

    Board { sensor, delay }
}
```

6. Main Entry Point

`src/main.rs`:

```rust
#![no_std]
#![no_main]

use panic_probe as _;
```

```rust
use defmt_rtt as _;

mod traits;
mod drivers;
mod platform;
mod app;

use app::logger::Logger;
use platform::board::init;

#[cortex_m_rt::entry]
fn main() -> ! {
    let mut board = init();
    let mut logger = Logger::new(board.sensor);

    loop {
        logger.poll();
        board.delay.delay_ms(5000u32);
    }
}
```

7. Build and Flash

Build and deploy the firmware:

```
cargo build --release
cargo flash --chip STM32F401RETx --release
```

Then open the log terminal:

```
cargo run --release
```

This runs the firmware and streams logs via RTT. You should see:

```
[INFO] Temp: 24.62°C
[INFO] Temp: 24.63°C
...
```

Every 5 seconds.

8. Test the Driver in Isolation

In **tests/tmp102_tests.rs:**

```
use embedded_hal_mock::i2c::{Mock as I2cMock,
Transaction};
use my_project::drivers::tmp102::Tmp102;

#[test]
fn reads_temperature_correctly() {
    let expectations =
[Transaction::write_read(0x48, vec![0x00],
vec![0x1A, 0x00])];
    let i2c = I2cMock::new(&expectations);

    let mut sensor = Tmp102::new(i2c, 0x48);
    let temp = sensor.read_temperature().unwrap();
    assert!((temp - 26.0).abs() < 0.1);
}
```

This ensures your driver logic is correct, even without a board.

Outcome

You now have a full embedded Rust project:

- Modular, testable, and portable
- Uses `embedded-hal` and `defmt`
- Sleeps between sensor reads
- Fully flashable, debuggable, and ready for deployment

This case study isn't just a template—it's a reliable architecture for building real embedded products. You can plug in new sensors, support new chips, and scale your logic—all with confidence that your code is structured, testable, and easy to maintain. That's what it means to ship embedded Rust firmware the right way.

Appendices

Appendix A: Rust Tooling and Build Profiles

Effective firmware development in Rust depends not just on writing correct code, but also on mastering the tooling that surrounds it. The Rust ecosystem offers a mature, powerful toolchain that supports reproducible builds, performance profiling, code size analysis, and cross-compilation—all essential when targeting constrained microcontroller platforms.

At the core of Rust development is `cargo`, the official build system and package manager. It orchestrates compilation, dependency resolution, release builds, and flashing. Understanding how to configure `cargo` and its profiles allows you to strike the right balance between speed, size, and debug visibility.

Rust uses *build profiles* to control how your code is compiled. These profiles determine optimization levels, panic strategies, debug symbol inclusion, and more.

There are three common profiles:

- `dev`: Used by default for `cargo build`, optimized for fast builds with full debug info
- `release`: Used by `cargo build --release`, optimized for speed and/or size
- `test`: Used for running tests, includes assertions and debug checks

In your `Cargo.toml`, you can configure the behavior of each profile. For embedded systems, the `release` profile is where most customization happens. A minimal, production-oriented configuration might look like this:

```
[profile.release]
opt-level = "z"
codegen-units = 1
lto = true
debug = true
panic = "abort"
```

This configuration prioritizes binary size (`opt-level = "z"`), enables link-time optimization (`lto = true`), and disables stack unwinding for smaller panic handling (`panic = "abort"`). The `debug = true` setting ensures symbol information is retained, which is useful for flashing tools and RTT logs, even in release builds.

Other essential tools include `rustup`, which manages Rust versions and targets. To compile for embedded architectures, you must add a target using:

```
rustup target add thumbv7em-none-eabihf
```

This adds support for ARM Cortex-M4 chips with hardware floating-point. You'll typically use this target in combination with a `.cargo/config.toml` file to streamline builds:

```
[build]
target = "thumbv7em-none-eabihf"

[target.thumbv7em-none-eabihf]
runner = "probe-rs run --chip STM32F401RETx"
```

This way, `cargo run` will compile for your microcontroller and flash it directly via `probe-rs`.

Understanding and using build profiles effectively lets you produce firmware that's efficient, testable, and suited to your deployment needs, without changing your code base.

Appendix B: Understanding Linker Scripts

Linker scripts define how your compiled code is placed into memory. In embedded systems, this is critical—your microcontroller has strict constraints on where code can live, how it starts, and what sections are mapped to flash or RAM.

Rust projects for embedded targets typically use a `memory.x` linker script to define the layout of the microcontroller's memory map. This script is required by `cortex-m-rt`, which provides startup code and exception vector setup.

Here is a basic `memory.x` file:

```
MEMORY
{
  FLASH : ORIGIN = 0x08000000, LENGTH = 512K
```

```
  RAM    : ORIGIN = 0x20000000, LENGTH = 128K
}
```

This tells the linker to place program code starting at address `0x08000000` (typical for flash) and use `0x20000000` for RAM. These addresses must match your chip's datasheet.

Sections in Rust (like `.text`, `.rodata`, `.bss`, `.data`) are placed into these memory regions by a separate linker script generated by `cortex-m-rt`. You can override or extend this behavior by customizing your linker script and passing it through `.cargo/config.toml`.

If your program uses interrupts or entry points defined via `#[entry]` and `#[interrupt]`, these are resolved by symbols placed into the interrupt vector table at the start of flash. The startup code sets the stack pointer and jumps to the main function from here.

Understanding linker scripts is vital when working with bootloaders, custom memory layouts, or low-level peripherals like DMA that require precise address placement.

Appendix C: Popular Crates in the Embedded Rust Ecosystem

The embedded Rust ecosystem is growing rapidly, and while it's still young compared to C-based frameworks, it already offers a solid set of crates for development, peripherals, and system integration. Knowing which crates to reach for will save you time and reduce duplication of effort.

- `cortex-m`: Provides access to ARM Cortex-M core peripherals and CPU-level features like interrupts, registers, and cycle counters. It's essential for all Cortex-M development.
- `cortex-m-rt`: Supplies the runtime setup, including vector table, reset handler, and stack configuration. It also defines the `#[entry]` and `#[exception]` macros for entry points.
- `embedded-hal`: Defines common hardware traits (I2C, SPI, GPIO, PWM, etc.) used by all driver crates. Most reusable drivers are written against this abstraction layer.
- `embedded-hal-async`: Provides experimental async-friendly traits for non-blocking firmware.
- `defmt`: A compact, log-optimized formatting system designed for embedded use. Pairs with `probe-run` or RTT for debug output.

- `rtt-target`: Enables RTT logging over the SWD interface, allowing efficient `println!`-like behavior without serial I/O.
- `panic-probe`, `panic-halt`, and `panic-abort`: Runtime panic handlers for different use cases. `panic-probe` integrates with `defmt`; `panic-halt` halts execution on panic; `panic-abort` simply triggers a CPU abort.
- `heapless`: Offers statically allocated data structures like `Vec`, `String`, and `RingBuffer` that don't require a dynamic allocator—critical in `no_std` environments.
- `smoltcp`, `embedded-nal`: Lightweight networking and abstraction libraries for TCP/IP and socket APIs in embedded environments.
- PAC and HAL crates: Automatically generated peripheral access crates (`stm32f4`, `nrf52840`, etc.) and higher-level hardware abstraction layers (`stm32f4xx-hal`, `nrf-hal`) used for initializing peripherals with safe idioms.

Choosing crates that adhere to community standards (especially `embedded-hal`) ensures you can build firmware that is portable, modular, and community-supported.

Appendix D: Troubleshooting Tips and Development FAQ

Embedded development is full of edge cases. Even with good tooling, things go wrong—builds fail, flashes stall, logs don't show up. This section outlines common issues and how to resolve them.

Why is my firmware not flashing?

Check the following:

- Is your target chip specified correctly in `.cargo/config.toml`?
- Is the probe recognized by `probe-rs-cli list`?
- Have you unlocked the chip if a bootloader or readout protection is enabled?

Why isn't my `println! ()` showing anything?

Rust's `std` I/O macros don't work in `no_std` environments. Use `defmt::info!` or RTT-based macros instead. Also, verify RTT is initialized and the host is running `cargo run` with probe support.

I get `HardFault`, how do I debug it?

Flash in debug mode and connect with `arm-none-eabi-gdb`. Use:

```
target remote :3333
monitor reset halt
backtrace
```

This shows where the fault occurred. Check for out-of-bounds memory access or invalid peripheral configuration.

My firmware works on one board but not another. Why?

Check for mismatches in:

- Clock settings
- GPIO alternate functions
- Memory sizes
- Pull-up/pull-down resistors on inputs

Use board schematics and verify peripheral initialization with an oscilloscope or logic analyzer if necessary.

Why is my binary so big?

Use `cargo bloat` to inspect size contributions. Common causes include:

- `core::fmt` via `format!` or `println!`
- Panics with backtraces
- Multiple crates depending on `std`-like APIs

Strip unused features, avoid heap allocations, and enable `opt-level = "z"`.

Why is my code not running after flash?

Ensure the reset vector and stack pointer are correctly placed. Check your `memory.x` file, and verify that `#[entry]` is applied only once. If using a bootloader, confirm that it correctly jumps to your application's reset handler.

By becoming fluent with Rust tooling, linker control, crate selection, and effective debugging strategies, you'll have everything you need to build stable, production-grade firmware that's as safe and expressive as it is efficient. These appendices serve as your go-to reference when things break, builds stall, or you're just trying to push your firmware that little bit further.